ZORA NEALE HURSTON

Paul Witcover

MELROSE SQUARE PUBLISHING COMPANY
LOS ANGELES, CALIFORNIA

PAUL WITCOVER is a College of William and Mary graduate whose short stories and poetry have appeared in various publications. He currently resides in New York City, where he is at work on a novel.

Senior Editor for Chelsea House
Black Americans of Achievement
Richard Rennert

Consulting Editors for Melrose Square
Raymond Friday Locke
James Neyland

Originally published by Chelsea House, New York, New Haven, Philadelphia © 1991 by Chelsea House

Cover Painting: Jesse Santos
Cover Design: Bill Skurski

ZORA NEALE HURSTON

MELROSE SQUARE
BLACK AMERICAN SERIES

CONTENTS

Chapter One

A Lot of Hope

WHEN ASPIRING WRITER Zora Neale Hurston entered Manhattan's Fifth Avenue Restaurant on May 1, 1925, she found the air crackling with excitement. More than three hundred well-dressed women and men circulated through the room, exchanging gossip, laughing, and nervously sipping cocktails. All awaited an important announcement. On this spring evening, the editors of the National Urban League's prestigious magazine, *Opportunity: A Journal of Negro Life*, were holding a dinner to reveal the winners of the publication's annual literary contest.

Zora Neale Hurston at the May 1, 1925, Opportunity *awards, which Arnold Rampersad called the "greatest gathering of black and white literati ever assembled in one room...."*

Under the leadership of editor Charles S. Johnson, *Opportunity* had become a major voice in the phenomenon known as the Harlem Renaissance. An artistic explosion among black writers and artists of the 1920s, the Renaissance produced a flood of dazzling prose and poetry. The movement—centered in the Harlem district of New York City, which boasted the largest black community in the nation—inspired blacks with new pride in their heritage, stirred widespread interest in African-American history and culture, and focused attention on literature as a means to preserve and celebrate the black experience.

Johnson had published Hurston's short story, "Drenched in Light," five months earlier, in the December 1924 issue of *Opportunity*. Recognizing her as a gifted writer, he then invited her to enter the *Opportunity* contest. She was quick to respond with *Color Struck*, a play, and "Spunk," another short story.

By that time, Hurston had already moved to Harlem from Washington, D.C., where she was a part-time student at Howard University and worked as a manicurist at a local barbershop. She had settled in "Harlem City," as she called the district, in January 1925 because she wanted to study writing at

Poet Countee Cullen, who would become one of Hurston's dearest friends, first met her at the 1925 Opportunity *magazine awards banquet in New York.*

one of New York's many universities. She also felt she might advance her career as a writer by meeting some of the city's cultural elite.

Manhattan's literary lions certainly seemed eager to honor a new generation of talented black Americans; they packed the Fifth Avenue Restaurant on the night of the *Opportunity* awards dinner. In his biography of poet Langston Hughes, Arnold Rampersad called the assemblage "the greatest gathering of black and white literati ever assembled in one room."

Among the literati were the contest's judges, who had read and evaluated more than 730 entries. The decision makers included such respected literary figures as drama critic Alexander Woollcott and playwright Eugene O'Neill, who was to win the Nobel Prize for literature in 1936. James Weldon Johnson, executive secretary of the National Association for the Advancement of Colored People (NAACP), was there, as was Jessie Fauset, a noted author and literary editor of the NAACP's magazine, *The Crisis*. So were two young poets with rapidly growing reputations, Langston Hughes and Countee Cullen— both, like Hurston, up for awards.

Some of the white writers and patrons of the arts who attended the dinner—critic and

Langston Hughes, another poet introduced to Hurston *at the* Opportunity *awards banquet, found himself bowled over by her colorful, non-stop repartee.*

novelist Carl Van Vechten, for example—genuinely respected black Americans' rich cultural traditions and admired their artistic achievements. Others had come simply because black artists were currently in vogue, and the Fifth Avenue Restaurant was the place to be on May 1. Perceiving the Harlem Renaissance as nothing more than the latest fad of the Jazz Age, this group knew little and cared less about the literary history unfolding before their eyes.

The gathering, which offered a chance to rub elbows with the cream of Manhattan's literary world, would have thrilled any young writer. It was precisely the opportunity that Hurston, who later wrote that she had arrived in New York "with $1.50, no job, no friends, and a lot of hope," had been waiting for.

By 1925, Hurston had learned a good deal about hope—and about turning hope into reality. Born in the all-black township of Eatonville, Florida, she had grown up in an atmosphere remarkably free of the racial prejudice and violence faced by most southern blacks.

In Eatonville, Hurston wrote later, she had learned "that I did not have to consider any racial group as a whole. God made them duck by duck and that was the only way I could see them. I learned that skins were no measure of what was inside people."

Hurston's early environment provided her with both advantages and disadvantages. It would give her lifelong, unshakable self-confidence, a strong sense of personal and racial worth, and a deep reverence for the traditional forms of African-American cultural expression. On the other hand, Eatonville's nonracist atmosphere failed to prepare Hurston for the world outside, where life was very different indeed.

Hurston had left Eatonville at the age of thirteen, after her mother's death. Shuttled from relative to relative, she began supporting herself at the age of fourteen. The following years, filled with hard work and uncertainty, had been difficult for a young woman who had learned to rely on her neighbors. In a world of strangers, Hurston discovered that she herself was the only person she could truly depend on.

Holding down a variety of menial and often humiliating jobs, Hurston managed to continue her education, a remarkable accomplishment for a young black woman in the early decades of the century. Somewhere along the way, she decided to become a writer. She had a passionate love of language, a keen ear for the music of speech, and memories of Eatonville that were begging to be written down.

A woman writer, particularly a black woman writer, had only the slimmest chance of getting published; but if anyone told Hurston that, she did not listen. In Eatonville, her mother had always encouraged her to "jump at the sun," and Hurston aimed to take that advice. So she wrote. And by 1925 she had written herself all the way to New York, to the *Opportunity* awards dinner and the outskirts of the Harlem Renaissance.

As the young writers waited anxiously for the prize winners to be announced, they introduced themselves to one another, talking shop and comparing notes. Outshining all the women in the crowd was the good-looking, flamboyantly dressed Zora Neale Hurston. She was "certainly the most amusing," Hughes noted later. "She was full of side-splitting anecdotes, humorous tales, and tragicomic stories, remembered out of her life in the South," he added. "She could make you laugh one minute and cry the next."

Describing Hurston in his 1977 biography, Robert E. Hemenway wrote: "Brown skinned, big boned, with freckles and high cheekbones, she was a striking woman; her dark brown eyes were both impish and intelligent, her voice was rich and black—with the map of Florida on her tongue." With her quick and easy laugh, her sharp wit, and her outrageous tales, Hurston charmed her fellow writers. Few could have guessed that beneath her carefree manner was a woman of steely determination, tempered by hardship and sorrow.

Keeping the year of her birth a closely guarded secret, Hurston regularly passed herself off as years younger than she really was. In truth, she was a decade older than many of her competitors at the awards dinner. Langston Hughes, for example, was twenty-three years old; Countee Cullen, twenty-four. Hurston had turned thirty-four in January, but she looked much younger, as photographs from the period show. Friends had often praised her acting ability; it is, perhaps, a testament to that skill that she managed to carry off the deception so successfully. Why it should have been so important to her is another matter. Hurston was and would continue to be extremely secretive, especially where her own history was concerned.

Hurston must have been disappointed when the *Opportunity* judges announced the winner of the contest's first prize: it was Langston Hughes, for his poem "The Weary Blues." Still, Hurston had reason to celebrate. She won second prize in two categories: fiction, for her short story, "Spunk," and drama, for her play, *Color Struck*.

Having already come quite a distance, Hurston was now on her way, and she would go farther still. But no matter how far her career took her—from the top of the best-seller lists to the depths of poverty and sickness—her heart never strayed far from Eatonville. One of the Greek myths she loved as a child was about a giant named Antaeus, a wrestler whose strength came from the earth of his native land. As long as Antaeus stood upon that ground, no one could defeat him. So it was with Zora Neale Hurston and Eatonville.

Fledging writer Zora Neale Hurston
swept into New York City
in 1925 with, she said,
"$1.50, no job, no
friends, and a lot of hope."
Her optimism proved well-founded.
Within a year of her arrival,
the ebullient Floridian had
taken the city's literary
establishment
by storm.

Chapter Two

Jumping at the Sun

Z ORA NEALE HURSTON, Lucy Ann and John Hurston's fifth child, was born on January 7, 1891, in Eatonville, Florida. January was hog-killing time, and it so happened that most of the Hurstons' neighbors— including old Aunt Judy, Lucy's midwife— had gone that day to a barbecue in a nearby community. Because John was also out of town, no one was present to assist with Zora's birth. As a result, Lucy, weak from blood loss, was forced to listen helplessly to the cries of her newborn girl.

Then a voice called from the door. It

Zora's father, John Hurston, was a popular preacher who moved his family to Eatonville, Florida, in the 1880s because it was built "all out of colored people."

belonged to a family friend, a white man who had stopped by to bring the Hurstons a ham. Rushing into the house, he cut Zora's umbilical cord with his hunting knife and set about caring for mother and child as best he could. By the time Aunt Judy arrived, Lucy had recovered enough to sit up in bed and hold her baby.

Zora's father, John Hurston, was preaching in another part of the state at the time of her birth. (Working both as a sharecropper and as a preacher, he was often away from home for months at a stretch.) When John heard he had a new daughter—his second—his reaction was somewhat less than joyful. As Zora Hurston was to note in her 1942 autobiography, *Dust Tracks on a Road*, her father "threatened to cut his throat when he got the news. It seems that one daughter was all he figured he could stand. Plenty more sons, but no more girl babies to wear out shoes and bring in nothing. I don't think he ever got over the trick he felt that I played on him by getting born a girl, and while he was off from home at that."

John Hurston and his daughter never grew close, but Zora would come to respect and admire many of her father's qualities. She made him, in fact, the central character in

John Hurston often preached at Zion Hope Baptist Church, but his daughter did not accept his formal religion. She wrote. "I do not expect God to...grant me advantages over my fellow men."

her first novel, *Jonah's Gourd Vine*, portraying him with a clear and sympathetic understanding. Although she saw many faults in her father, Zora recognized him as a remarkable man who had beaten tough odds to make something of himself.

John Hurston had spent the first two decades of his life picking cotton for white farmers in Alabama, but the years of hard labor had broken neither his body nor his spirit. He had found the time to learn how to read and write, and he had become an excellent carpenter. He had also been "called" to preach the gospel, which he did in a rousing poetic style.

A handsome man of imposing physical presence, John Hurston was so strong, it was said, that he once knocked out a mule with a single punch. And he was a natural leader; men followed him willingly. Unfortunately for his wife, so did women. Even after he married Lucy Potts, a pretty, fourteen-year-old Alabaman, when he was twenty, John continued to see other women. He regarded his unfaithfulness as no great sin as long as he provided for his family, which he was always careful to do.

Lucy Hurston was as slight of body as her husband was large. But she proved more

Youngsters playing on a summer afternoon in Hurston's home-town of Eatonville, Florida. "In my family," she later recalled, "it was not ladylike for girls to play with boys."

than his match when it came to intelligence
and determination. Disowned by the relatively well-to-do Potts family for marrying the
handsome sharecropper from "over the
creek," Lucy wasted no time regretting what
she had lost. Instead, she worked hard to
build a future for herself and her growing
family.

By the time Lucy Hurston's third child was
born, her husband had grown thoroughly
tired of life in the Alabama cottonfields.
"There was no rise to the thing," Zora
Hurston noted later. Temporarily leaving his
wife and family, John Hurston went off to
search for something better. On his travels,
his youngest daughter wrote in her autobiography, he heard rumors about "folks building
a town"—Eatonville, in central Florida—"all
out of colored people. It seemed like a good
place to go."

It was indeed. The area's rich soil made for
fine farming. The lakes teemed with fish. The
trees bore oranges, grapefruit, tangerines,
and guavas. The summers were hot, the win-
ters mild. After living there for a year, John
Hurston sent for his wife and children,
bought five acres of land, and built an eight-
room house. His life as a sharecropper had
come to an end.

Eatonville offered both Lucy and John Hurston the opportunity to realize their ambitions, although in traditional ways: Lucy within the family structure and John outside it. She imbued all eight of her children—especially Zora, admittedly her favorite—with a strong sense of self-worth and a deep love of knowledge. John, who took on the responsibility of running a church, also wrote Eatonville's laws and served three terms as the town's mayor.

Incorporated in 1886, twenty-one years after the end of the Civil War, Eatonville was the first all-black American community to win the right of self-government. This was no white town's "black backside," nor was it a settlement where slavery lingered under a different name and blacks lived in poverty "on the wrong side of the tracks." Eatonville was a unique municipality, one where traditional black culture not only survived but flourished. Surrounded on all sides by the choking weeds of racism, Eatonville bloomed like a rare and beautiful flower, a black rose.

At no time was the special character of Eatonville more evident than on the night when its residents heard screams from the nearby woods. It was late, and one of their neighbors, Jim Watson, had not yet come home. No one knew for sure, but it was feared he was being tortured, or even murdered, by members of the Ku Klux Klan, the most notorious white supremacist group in America. Led by John Hurston, the men of Eatonville picked up their shotguns and marched into the woods.

As it turned out, the cries were coming from a local white man who was being beaten for offending the Klan. But the men of Eatonville had not known that. They had faced potential death at the hands of the Klan in order to help a neighbor. Those were the kind of people who had dared to build a black town in the segregated South. Proud of their community, the men and women of Eatonville taught their children to take similar pride in their town and in their race.

Black Americans had founded Eatonville because they were denied the opportunity to live as free and equal citizens in white communities. As an adult, Zora Hurston saw this as good coming out of evil; "hitting a straight lick with a crooked stick" was how she put it. She considered herself not only her parents' daughter but the daughter of her town as well. And like that town, she would make the best of a bad situation. She would overlook the crookedness of her stick and concentrate

Hurston attended Eatonville's Hungerford School (founded in 1889) until she was thirteen years old. It was the only school for blacks in central Florida.

on hitting straight licks.

Zora sought to get things straight even as a child; she loved to ask direct questions that her parents could never seem to answer: questions about the why of things, about beginnings and ends. From the top of the great chinaberry tree at the front gate of her home, she studied the horizon and wondered what the edge of the world was like, "whether it was sort of tucked under like the hem of a dress, or just a sharp drop off into nothingness." She vowed to find out.

The road to the horizon—by way of Orlando—ran right past the Hurstons' front yard. Perched on the gate post, Zora would often hail passing motorists—invariably white in those early days of the automobile— and boldly hitch a lift for a half-mile or so, telling stories or singing songs in exchange for the ride. If her parents caught her at this pastime, Zora was sure to get a whipping. But nothing could stop the little girl from following what she later called her "inside urge to go places."

Zora's mother believed that this urge had come from an unknown enemy who had sprinkled her doorstep with "travel dust" on the day Zora was born. Such a curse could not easily be undone; it was best, she felt, just to accept it.

But John Hurston did not share his wife's tolerance for Zora's independent ways. He believed it was his duty to beat such dangerous urges out of Zora before the white folks did so permanently. As Hurston would write of her father's views: "It did not do for Negroes to have too much spirit. He was always threatening to break mine or kill me in the attempt. He predicted dire things for me. The white folks were not going to stand for it. I was going to be hung before I got grown."

John Hurston's words indicated no passive acceptance of white racism; proud of his heritage, he conceded inferiority to no one. Nevertheless, as a practical man, he knew no other way to protect his boisterous child from the harsh and unforgiving racism of the South than by teaching her to act as a black girl was expected to act—by blacks as well as whites.

But Zora was never willing to conform to anyone's racist or sexist expectations. And in her mother, Zora found a powerful ally in her battle to remain true to herself. "Jump at the sun," Lucy Hurston said to her children. "We might not land on the sun," Zora noted later, "but at least we would get off the ground."

Southerners swap yarns at a general store, an emporium much like the one Joe Clarke ran in Eatonville. Eavesdropping on the adults

gathered on Clarke's porch, young Zora Neale Hurston heard many of the tales she would later weave into her novels and short stories.

Whenever John Hurston started in on Zora, Lucy Hurston was there to step between them. "She conceded that I was impudent and given to talking back," recalled her daughter, "but she didn't want to 'squinch my spirit' too much for fear that I would turn out to be a mealy-mouthed rag doll by the time I got grown."

Zora—who would never display the slightest resemblance to a rag doll—appreciated her mother's support. She also valued the guidance of another ally: the white man who had helped to bring her into the world. She spent many summer afternoons with this elderly friend, fishing and talking about life. In her autobiography, Hurston recalled samples of his advice: "Any time you catch folks lying," he said one day, "they are skeered of something. Lying is dodging. People with guts don't lie. They tell the truth and then if they have to, they fight it out."

Hurston's plain-speaking friend also cautioned her against making any threat she could not carry out. "Give 'em what you promise 'em," he said, "and they'll look up to you even if they hate your guts. Don't worry over that part. Somebody is going to hate you anyhow, don't care what you do." Emphasizing his point, the old man added,

"And while I'm on the subject, don't you never let nobody spit on you or kick you. Anybody who takes a thing like that ain't worth the powder and shot it takes to kill 'em, hear?"

Zora heard. "Yessir," she responded.

Young Zora was thus confronted with contradictory advice from the adults she respected most. Her father, a brave and successful man, ordered her to be meek and self-effacing in order to placate the whites. Her trusted white friend, on the other hand, urged her to stand up for herself and fight for what she believed in. As she grew up, Zora Hurston would absorb both these philosophies without ever truly integrating them.

She would also grow up to be something of a loner. Stronger than the other girls her own age, Zora always seemed to be hurting someone by accident. And she had little patience for traditional little-girl playthings. "Dolls caught the devil around me," she recalled later. "They got into fights and leaked sawdust." She liked to roughhouse with the neighborhood boys, with whom she could give as good as she got, although her parents frowned on such unladylike behavior. Scorning the girls, yet forbidden to play with the boys, Zora took refuge in her own fertile imagination.

From odds and ends around the house, she fashioned Miss Corn Shuck, Mr. Sweet Smell, the Reverend Door Knob, and a supporting cast of Spool People—all characters in a long-running private drama. She also invented a secret life for a meek old man who lived alone on the shore of nearby Lake Belle. In her fantasy, the seemingly harmless fisherman turned at night into an alligator king who walked on water "with thousands on thousands of his subject-'gators moving silently along beside him and behind him in an awesome and mighty convoy."

Sometimes, Zora shared her imaginary world with her mother. She told Lucy Hurston about the bird in the garden; his colorful tail was so long, said Zora, that it reached from the top of the tall pine tree to the ground. When she climbed his "blue and pink and red and green" tail, the bird told her he had come especially to talk to her. She also talked to the lake, which invited her to walk on its surface.

"I could see all the fish and things swimming around under me, and they all said hello, but none of them bothered me," she told her mother. "Wasn't that nice?"

Her mother said it was.

"Mother never tried to break me," Hurston

recalled as an adult. "She'd listen sometimes, and sometimes she wouldn't. But she never seemed displeased."

Zora Hurston also recalled having "visions" from the time she was seven years old. As a little girl—and even as an adult—she believed that these extraordinarily vivid dreams revealed her future. "I was weighed down with a power I did not want," she wrote in her autobiography. "I had knowledge before its time."

Zora's visions increased her feeling of separation from her peers. "I played, fought and studied with other children, but always I stood apart," she recalled. "A cosmic loneliness was my shadow. Nothing and nobody around me really touched me. It is one of the blessings of this world that few people see visions and dream dreams."

Zora, of course, had begun the process of becoming a writer.

Zora's discovery of books pushed her farther along the path to her future career. Lucy Hurston had taught all her children to read before they started school. Zora, who had fallen in love with books at once, read every volume she could find "from lid to lid," as she put it later. When she was in the fifth grade, her teacher once asked her to read aloud for two white women visiting the school. Her impassioned reading from a book of Greek mythology so impressed the visitors that they sent her a whole box of books, more than she had ever dreamed of owning.

Among Zora's new treasures were *Gulliver's Travels*, the fairy tales of Hans Christian Andersen and the Brothers Grimm, and the adventure stories of Rudyard Kipling and Robert Louis Stevenson. Best of all were the collections of Greek, Roman, and Norse mythology, with their stories so different from—and yet strangely similar to—the folktales she had grown up hearing.

Zora's interest in books impressed her elders. Relatives and teachers were especially pleased to see her reading the Bible—not suspecting that she was attracted more by its exciting tales than its spiritual content.

Picking up her mother's well-worn Bible one day, Zora chanced on the story of David. The Old Testament hero, she wrote later, "was doing some mighty smiting, and I got interested. David went here and he went there, and no matter where he went, he smote 'em hip and thigh. Then he sung songs to his harp awhile, and went out and smote some more. Not one time did David stop and preach about sins and things. All David wanted to know from God was who to kill and when. He took care of the other details himself. Never a quiet moment. I liked him a lot."

Eventually, Zora's interest in books took her away from the life of the town. "In a way, this early reading gave me great anguish through all my childhood and adolescence. My soul was with the gods and my body in the village," she recalled. "Raking back yards and carrying out chamber pots were not the work of [heroes]. I wanted to be away from that drabness and to stretch my limbs in some mighty struggle."

Despite her impatience to enter the wider world, Zora loved Eatonville. She was particularly drawn to the front porch of Joe Clarke's general store, which she called "the heart and spring" of the town. She was not allowed to join the adults who congregated around the store, but whenever her parents sent her there, she managed to move very slowly, "to allow whatever was being said to hang in my ear."

What was being said sometimes proved as exciting as anything Zora could read about or imagine. It was not just town gossip, although there was plenty of that, much of it frankly sexual; men and women swapped boasts and friendly insults in terms young

Zora understood far better than the speakers guessed.

Talk at Joe Clarke's store also included "lying sessions"—folktales about how the world had come to be, about why some people were black and others white, about God and the devil, about animals that spoke human language. For the most part unwritten, these stories had been passed down among blacks for generations, sometimes changing in certain details but always retaining a life-affirming core of spiritual truth—"that which the soul lives by," Zora Hurston said.

Deriving in part from African traditions, in part from the experience of slavery and the influence of Christianity, the stories were in many ways like those in Zora's mythology books. But these folktales were not the unchanging, written myths of white people; these were the myths of African Americans, passed from mouth to mouth, always free to change and to grow. These myths were still alive.

Zora devoured these folk legends; as an adult, she would remember not only every word but the gestures and movements with which the stories were told. At the time, of course, she did not realize she was helping to preserve an ancient oral tradition; nor did she know that all-black Eatonville provided a unique sanctuary for such cultural traditions. She only knew that she loved hearing her neighbors tell stories.

The young Zora saw little difference between the folktales she heard on Joe Clarke's porch and the stories she made up herself. But as she grew older, she would discover that there was a difference after all: folklore is the collective expression of a people, fiction the creation of an individual. Never comfortable with this division, Hurston would one day strive to combine fiction and folklore, group and individual. In so doing, she would carve her own niche in American literary history.

Chapter Three

A Dry Season

IN 1904 WHEN ZORA Hurston was thirteen years old, her mother caught a cold she could not shake. Her cough grew worse and worse. When every breath became a struggle, she took to her bed. Soon she lacked the strength to leave it.

Small towns contain few secrets, and illness is not one of them. When neighbors came to offer sympathy and help, they saw that Lucy Hurston was more than just sick. She was dying.

Grief, guilt, fear, and denial are among the universal human responses to death; all cul-

Abandoned by her father, Hurston spent most of her young adult life having to fend for herself. She was about twenty when this photograph was taken.

tures have developed rituals to express these emotions in an orderly and positive way. In Eatonville, people believed that a pillow beneath the head of a dying person prolonged the final agonies; therefore, the pillow was always removed. The sickroom mirror had to be covered lest the reflection of the corpse attach itself to the glass. The clock, too, was hooded; otherwise, the glance of the departing soul would freeze it forever at the instant of death. These practices and beliefs, rooted in the common folklore of black communities in the South and the Caribbean, provided a powerful comfort to the townspeople.

But the thought of them did not comfort Lucy Hurston. Perhaps hoping to prolong her life—as if the rituals were the cause of death instead of a response to it—she meant to reject them. On September 18, she called Zora to her bedside. No one, she said, was to remove her pillow or cover the mirror and clock. Would Zora make sure her wishes were carried out? The teenager, pleased to be trusted with such an important request, promised that she would.

Lucy Hurston took a turn for the worse that same evening. Zora, who had gone outside for a breath of air, entered her mother's room in time to see some of the local women moving the sickbed to face the east, toward the rising sun—another custom believed to ease the sufferings of the dying. One woman reached for the pillow beneath Lucy's head. Others began to cover the clock and mirror.

Zora rushed to stop them. "Don't cover up that clock!" she cried. "Leave that looking-glass like it is! Lemme put Mama's pillow back where it was!"

But no one heeded her cries. Her father dragged her back and held on tight. Lucy's eyes seemed to plead with her, but there was nothing Zora could do. "Just then," she wrote later, "Death finished his prowling through the house on his padded feet and entered the room. He bowed to Mama in his way, and she made her manners and left us to act out our ceremonies over unimportant things."

In that moment, which would haunt her memory for the rest of her life, Zora Hurston got her first real taste of the power of folklore. Although she was too young to understand fully, she saw that the customs of the community outweighed even a dying woman's last wish; confronted by the mystery of death, it was the living who needed protection and reassurance.

Locked in her father's strong arms while Lucy Hurston gasped out her final breaths,

Jacksonville, Florida (shown here in 1905), delivered a rude shock to adolescent Hurston. Sent to school in the segregated city,

the young woman from Eatonville discovered that she was no longer Zora. "I was now," she wrote later, "a little colored girl."

Zora knew she had failed her mother. "That moment was the end of a phase in my life," she wrote afterward. "I was old before my time with grief of loss, of failure, and of remorse. No matter what the others did, my mother had put her trust in me. She had felt that I could and would carry out her wishes, and I had not.... It seemed as she died that the sun went down on purpose to flee away from me."

Lucy Hurston was buried the next day. The day after that, Zora's older brother and sister, Bob and Sarah, took the train to Jacksonville, where they were both attending school. Zora joined them two weeks later. She would return to Eatonville many times in the years to come, but she would never again consider it home.

Jacksonville, a bustling city located on the St. John's River in northeast Florida, was as different from Eatonville as could be imagined. Zora had never been to such a big and busy place. But it was different from Eatonville in more than just size: Jacksonville was rigorously segregated. The names of Joe Clarke and other prominent Eatonville townspeople were not known or honored there. Jacksonville was Jim Crow's town.

For a young girl raised in an atmosphere

where, Hurston said, "white people differed from colored...only because they rode through town and never lived there," Jacksonville raised some disturbing questions. In her essay, "How It Feels To Be Colored Me," the adult Hurston said, "I left Eatonville, the town of the oleanders, as Zora. When I disembarked from the riverboat at Jacksonville, she was no more.... I was now a little colored girl."

But Zora's harsh discovery of racism—right on the heels of her mother's death—failed to make her bitter. In her mind, Eatonville remained the norm, Jacksonville the exception. She regarded the "funny ways" of the local whites as strange variations in human behavior, a cause for amusement or sympathy, but not for self-pity. Zora Hurston was beginning to think with the objectivity of the folklorist and anthropologist she would become.

In her new school, Zora continued to excel in those subjects that interested her. "Lessons had never worried me," she noted, "although arithmetic still seemed an unnecessary evil." She won first prize in a citywide spelling bee—among black schools only, of course— and began to make friends with the other girls. She even learned, she said later, "how not to be bored at prayer-meeting—you could always write notes if you didn't go to sleep." Her only difficulty, she recalled, was that she was "rated as sassy"; teachers "hated back-talk worse than barbed-wire pie."

Two months into Zora's first term in Jacksonville, her sister Sarah decided to return to Eatonville. From there she wrote Zora with disturbing news: their father had remarried. The arrival of Sarah, who had always been John Hurston's favorite child, distressed his new wife, who soon forced the young woman out of the house and into an unhappy marriage. (For Sarah's husband, Hurston noted later, "we all wished a short sickness and a quick funeral.")

Almost as bad as her sister's fate—at least from Zora's point of view—her father started to fall behind in her tuition payments. In order to remain at school, she worked as a maid and kitchen helper. At the end of the year, Zora waited for her father to come and pick her up. Days, then weeks, passed, but he never showed up.

At last, the school principal received a letter from John Hurston; it suggested that the school adopt his daughter. The usually stern principal softened a little as she read Zora this "crumbling news," then told the teenager

A 1906 portrait of the second Mrs. John Hurston and her husband. Jealous of her predecessor's offspring, she hustled them out of the house as soon as possible.

that adoption was out of the question. She gave her money to get home and bade her farewell. Zora returned to Eatonville alone.

"So I came back to my father's house, which was no longer home. The very walls were gummy with gloom," Zora Hurston wrote in her autobiography. She found her father a changed man. Without Lucy Hurston to spur him on, he seemed content with what he had already accomplished, not only unwilling to assume new responsibilities but eager to lighten the load.

The new Mrs. Hurston took no interest in her husband's ambition or his children. By the time Zora got home, the four oldest had already left, and one by one, the four younger children were packed off to live with friends of Lucy Hurston.

The families that housed Zora had little interest in sending her to school. "People who had no parents," she noted, "could not afford to sit around on school benches wearing out what clothes they had." After a year of moving from one house to another, she went to work. Yet her independent attitude made it hard for her to keep the jobs—most of them as a maid or a waitress—she landed. "Sometimes I didn't suit the people," she recalled. "Sometimes the people didn't suit me. Sometimes my insides tortured me so that I was restless and unstable. I was doing none of the things I wanted to do..., and it was tearing me to pieces."

Hurston spent at least five years wandering from one job to another, living from hand to mouth, never able to afford clothes or, even worse, books. "There is something about poverty that smells like death," she observed in her autobiography. "Dead dreams dropping off the heart like leaves in a dry season and rotting around the feet; impulses smothered too long in the fetid air of underground caves. The soul lives in a sickly air. People can be slave-ships in shoes."

Hurston's spirit was not broken by adversity; she never stopped searching for a way to live better. But how to break free of the cycle of dead-end jobs that had entrapped her ever since she left Jacksonville in 1905?

The answer came out of nowhere. In 1910, a friend told Hurston that the star of a traveling operetta company, then on a swing through the South, needed a lady's maid. "It's a swell job if you can get it, Zora," the friend said. "I think you can." Her guess was correct.

Like most of the events in the first twenty-six years of her life, it is very difficult to date exactly when Hurston joined the operetta

Hurston's 1917 enrollment in Baltimore's Morgan Academy gave her spirits a much-needed boost. Although she had received little formal education, her Morgan entrance

examination so impressed the dean, William Pickens, that he gave her credit for two years of high school. He also found a live-in job for her with one of the trustees.

company. She herself is responsible for much of the problem, consistently (and probably deliberately) obscuring the facts. In some cases—her own birth, for example—she cited different dates at different times. In her autobiography, she scrupulously avoided mentioning any dates at all.

Hurston's experience with the operetta troupe is no exception. Based on the best available evidence, which establishes her birth date as January 7, 1891, she joined the troupe in late 1910. In her autobiography, however, she wrote that she stayed with the troupe for only eighteen months before leaving to enroll in Morgan Academy, a secondary school in Baltimore, Maryland.

Morgan's records indicate that Hurston entered its student body in 1917. This creates a seven-year gap, a period in which it is impossible to account for Hurston's movements. According to biographer Robert Hemenway, "At least one member of her family thinks she might have secretly married sometime during this period." But this tantalizing possibility remains unproved.

In any case, Hurston thoroughly enjoyed her stint with the traveling company, which specialized in the musicals of Gilbert and Sullivan. Her employer, a beautiful young blonde singer Hurston identified only as "Miss M," took an instant liking to the young black woman from Florida. "Well, Zora," the woman said at the beginning of their relationship, "I pay ten dollars a week and expenses. You think that will do?"

"I almost fell over," Hurston recalled. "Ten dollars each and every week! Was there that much money in the world sure enough?... 'Yes, ma'am!' I shouted."

Hurston soon became the company pet, affectionately teased, confided in, and counted upon by cast and crew alike. She traveled with the troupe until Miss M announced that she was getting married and leaving the tour. Hurston should leave too, said her employer. "She thought that I should not be working at all," Hurston wrote later. "I ought to be in school. She said she thought I had a mind."

The company had just performed in Baltimore. Miss M, Hurston reported, "inquired about [local] schools, gave me a big bearful hug and what little money she could spare and told me to keep in touch with her."

The curtain falls. What happens to Hurston during the next seven years remains enshrouded, at least for now, in mystery.

When the curtain rises again, seven years have passed.

Chapter Four

Urge to Write

IN 1917, ZORA HURSTON'S desire to complete her education burned more brightly than ever. At twenty-six, she had seen enough of the world to know what kind of life a poor, uneducated black woman could expect. "I took a firm grip on the only weapon I had—hope—and set my feet," she wrote later. "Maybe everything would be all right from now on. Maybe. Well, I put on my shoes and I started."

Hurston's first step took her to night school in Baltimore. Working as a waitress during the day, she studied English literature in the

Hurston (center) relaxes with friends at Howard, the prestigious Washington, D.C., university she entered in 1919. She was a decade older than her classmates.

evenings. High praise from one of her most admired teachers encouraged her to go further: after a few months, she applied for admission to Morgan Academy, the high school division of Baltimore's Morgan State College.

Dean William Pickens of Morgan was so impressed with Hurston's entrance examination that he gave her two years of high school credit. He also found her a live-in job with one of the college trustees, a clergyman whose invalid wife needed a companion. To Hurston's delight, the family had a well-stocked library. "I waded in," she later reported.

Most of Morgan's students came from well-to-do, middle-class black families. "Well, here was this class of pretty girls and snappy boys," Hurston recalled. "And here I was, with my face looking like it had been chopped out of a knot of pine wood with a hatchet on somebody's day off, sitting up in the middle of all this pretty." Making the young Floridian feel even more conspicuous was her wardrobe: one dress, one pair of tan shoes, and one set of underwear. Nevertheless, said Hurston, "Nobody shoved me around." Her fellow students, in fact, accepted her quickly; the boys asked her out and the girls loaned her clothes.

Hurston shone at her studies, proving so good in English and history that she soon became a substitute teacher in these subjects. She was, however, less successful in mathematics; the subject was always her downfall. "Why should A be minus B? Who the devil was X anyway? I could not even imagine. I still do not know," she joked in her autobiography.

During Hurston's first year at Morgan, she received word that her father had been killed in an automobile accident. Never reconciled with him in life, Hurston found that she could spare him some understanding, if not forgiveness, now that he was gone. "In reality, my father was the baby of the family," she wrote later. "With my mother gone and nobody to guide him, life had not hurt him, but it had turned him loose to hurt himself."

Hurston graduated from Morgan Academy in June 1918. She spent the next year in the preparatory division of Howard University in Washington, D.C.; in the fall of 1919, she became a freshman at Howard, the institution she proudly called "the capstone of Negro education in the world." She would attend Howard intermittently over the next five years.

Hurston's college years coincided with a period of unprecedented change for black

Returning from the European front after World War I, the all-black 15th Infantry Regiment marches up New York City's Fifth Avenue. But discrimination only became worse.

Americans. Setting the stage for the Harlem Renaissance of the 1920s was the previous decade's so-called "Great Migration," a vast northward shift of the nation's black population. Accelerated by World War I, which created severe labor shortages in the northern industrial cities, the migration brought more than one million blacks into the North. Many settled in Harlem.

At the same time, black leaders throughout the United States were revising their strategy for combating racial oppression. A turning point in this campaign occurred when black veterans returned to America after World War I and discovered they remained second-class citizens: even though these men had risked their lives for their country, the government would still not grant them the same rights and privileges as whites. Militant views began to replace the slow, patient approach to full citizenship, long preached by educator Booker T. Washington and other black moderates.

The leading voice in this fight for racial equality belonged to W.E.B. Du Bois, who had eloquently opposed Washington since the turn of the century. Instrumental in founding the National Association for the Advancement of Colored People (NAACP) in May 1909, Du Bois was editor of *The Crisis*, the organization's outspoken journal, which began publication in 1910. The journal's aim, Du Bois said, was to "record important happenings and movements in the world which bear on the great problem of interracial relations." *The Crisis* quickly garnered a large following, and by 1920 its circulation had surged to 100,000 copies.

As the journal's appeal grew, Du Bois' theory of the "Talented Tenth," which called on the educated black elite to provide forceful leadership for the black masses, found a receptive audience among the emerging black artists and intellectuals of the postwar years. These young women and men, most of them from middle-class backgrounds, were eager to assume the responsibility of advancing their race, with or without the help of white America.

The turbulent postwar years also saw the rise of Marcus Mosiah Garvey, leader of the Universal Negro Improvement Association (UNIA), which by 1919 claimed a worldwide membership of two million. In contrast to the scholarly Du Bois, Garvey was a flamboyant public figure who addressed not merely the Talented Tenth but the entire black population. His was a message of black nationalism and economic self-sufficiency; among other

Edited by W.E.B. Du Bois, The Crisis *magazine raised a strong voice for equal rights and became a subject of intense discussion among Hurston and her college friends.*

enterprises, Garvey founded the Black Star Line, a steamship company owned by UNIA members and dedicated to the repatriation of blacks to Africa.

Viewed by Du Bois and others as a dangerous trickster, Garvey nonetheless won a large and dedicated following prior to his 1923 conviction on charges of mail fraud. The UNIA quickly crumbled without its leader, but the issues Garvey had raised would not disappear so quickly.

Exposed to these exciting new messages and ideas at Howard, Hurston spent many nights discussing them with other thoughtful students and professors. She wrote for the school paper and became a member of Stylus, the campus literary club sponsored by philosophy professor Alain Locke and dramatic arts instructor Montgomery Gregory. Regarding themselves as members of Du Bois' Talented Tenth, Locke and Gregory were eager to bring the spirit of the Harlem Renaissance, with its pride in black America's cultural heritage, to the relatively staid Howard community.

Hurston also found time for non-intellectual matters: in 1920, she fell in love with Herbert Sheen, a Howard student preparing for a medical career. How did she know she had fallen in love? "When I fall *in*, I can feel the bump," she explained in her autobiography. "That is a fact and I would not try to fool you. Love may be a sleepy, creeping thing with some others, but it is a mighty wakening thing with me. I feel the jar and I know it from my head on down."

Hurston was, she said, "carried away" by this good-looking, piano-playing young man from Illinois. "For the first time since my mother's death," she said, "there was someone who felt really close and warm to me." Leaving Howard in 1921, Sheen went on to Chicago, where he entered medical school in 1924. Yet he and Hurston stayed in close contact during those years and often discussed marriage.

To support her schooling, Hurston worked as a manicurist at a Washington, D.C., barbershop. Like many such establishments in the nation's capital, George Robinson's shop was owned and staffed by blacks but served only whites. One day, however, a black man walked into the shop and asked for a haircut and shave. One of the barbers told him the establishment was for whites only. But the man refused to leave. The Constitution, he said, guaranteed him the right to have his hair cut in any barbershop he chose.

This argument did not go over well with the

The main building of Howard University, one of the nation's oldest and most distinguished institutions of black higher education.

Extremely proud of her affiliation with Howard, Hurston called it "the capstone of Negro education in the world."

fifteen black employees or the half-dozen white customers. In a rare display of interracial cooperation, they joined forces and tossed the intruder out of the shop. Hurston did not participate in the action, but she had no sympathy for the would-be customer. With candor that would be surprising coming from almost anyone but Zora Neale Hurston, she discussed the episode in *Dust Tracks on a Road*.

"I wanted him thrown out, too," she admitted. "My business was threatened." It might have been "a beautiful thing," Hurston said, if the black employees had stood by the man; but it would also have put the shop out of business. "It would have…made the headlines for a day," she wrote. "Then we could have all gone home to our unpaid rents and bills."

After the incident, Hurston thought long and hard about its meaning. She realized that by protecting her livelihood, she had helped perpetuate segregation, a system she knew she should oppose. "Offhand, you might say that we fifteen Negroes should have felt the racial thing and served [the black man]," she said. But, she added, "There is always something fiendish and loathsome about a person who threatens to deprive you of your way of making a living." The episode, she concluded, demonstrated one simple, "human-like" fact:

"Self-interest rides over all sorts of lines." It was a conclusion she was to draw many times in the future.

Despite the realities of Jim Crow America, Hurston never defined herself as a member of a wronged or exploited race. In her 1928 essay, "How It Feels to Be Colored Me," she wrote, "I am not tragically colored. There is no great sorrow dammed up in my soul, nor lurking behind my eyes. I do not belong to the sobbing school of Negrohood who hold that nature somehow has given them a lowdown dirty deal and whose feelings are all hurt about it."

Hurston, who would write with moving eloquence of the pernicious evils of racism, would become a tireless and courageous champion of black culture and folklore. But when it came to the politics of racial equality, she was first and foremost an individualist who based her beliefs on her own unique circumstances. Often ignoring established facts and popular wisdom, she would be perceived by some critics as naive or even reactionary.

Hurston, whose literary ambitions were encouraged by Howard University's Alain Locke, published her first short story, "John Redding Goes to Sea," in the May 1921 issue of *Stylus*, the Howard literary magazine.

"John Redding," while no masterpiece, fore-shadows much of Hurston's later fiction. In this work, she struggled to express the essence of her experiences in Eatonville, where she had felt both like a member of the community and an outsider, set apart by her feelings of "cosmic loneliness."

Hurston's first story deals with the contrast between wanting to belong and wanting to escape. Attached by strong family ties to his Florida hometown—which closely resembles Eatonville—John Redding longs to go to sea, hoping to find the place "where the sky touch-es the ground." He finally achieves his goal, but ironically only in death. Expressing the author's deep personal feelings, the roots-*vs*-flight theme also spoke directly to the black experience in white America. In her subse-quent work, Hurston would return to this theme again and again.

Hurston improved rapidly as a writer, as if making up for lost time. "Drenched in Light," the short story she published in 1924 in *Opportunity*, is in every way the work of a mature artist and remains one of the finest stories she ever wrote. Largely autobiographi-cal, "Drenched in Light" is once again set in an Eatonville-like town. At the story's center is Isis Watts, a "small brown girl" who loves nothing better than to "sit atop of the gate post and hail the passing vehicles."

As Hurston once did, Isis dreams of journeying to the horizon. Her bright and carefree spirit stands in stark contrast to that of her grandmother, who believes that young girls should sit still and silent and constantly threatens Isis with a whipping for refusing to obey.

The story consists of a series of episodes linked together by Isis' vibrant character and her almost magical power to transmit joy and happiness. Like the Egyptian goddess whose name she shares, Isis brings new life to the people around her. Although she is unconscious of her power, she is "drenched in light" and cannot help but spread that light to others.

At the story's end, three bored white tourists—two men and a woman—give Isis a ride in their car. The men quickly dismiss her, but the woman, more sensitive, is able to see the light that fills Isis and to recognize her own lack of, and need for, that living light: "She looked hungrily ahead of her and spoke into space rather than to anyone in the car. 'I would like just a little of her sunshine to soak into my soul. I would like that a lot.'"

When Hurston sent "Drenched in Light" to

Charles Johnson, the *Opportunity* editor realized he was onto something: the author of this concise, powerful work of fiction was clearly one of the promising young writers he was looking for. He promptly published the story and wrote Hurston what she called "a kind letter." He "said something about New York," she recalled. "So beginning to feel the urge to write, I wanted to be in New York." In 1925, she went.

Hurston (right), who once said, "Dolls caught the devil around me," poses with a college friend in 1920. This photograph was taken by Hurston's college sweetheart, a handsome young medical student named Herbert Sheen.

Chapter Five

Renaissance!

Zora HURSTON COULD NOT have picked a better time to arrive in New York. In 1925, the Harlem Renaissance was in full swing. All over the city, from Harlem itself to midtown to Greenwich Village, African-American culture occupied center stage. Ethel Waters sang at the Plantation Club and Fletcher Henderson led his band at the Roseland Ballroom. Jean Toomer, Claude McKay, Countee Cullen, and Langston Hughes wrote poetry. Walter White, Jessie Fauset, and Nella Larson wrote novels. Aaron Douglas and Archibald Motley painted murals and portraits. Dramas and musicals fea-

Alain Locke, Hurston's mentor, friend, and eventual critic, came to the Harlem Renaissance with impressive credentials: he was the first African-American Rhodes scholar at Oxford University.

turing black performers played to packed houses, not only in Harlem's popular Cotton Club but in the glittering theaters of Broadway.

In a city whose motto might have been "Anything Goes," Hurston became a natural star. With her uninhibited style, flamboyant clothes, and vast repertoire of colorful stories, she was regarded, according to Langston Hughes, as "a perfect book of entertainment in herself." By simply retelling the stories she had learned on the porch of Joe Clarke's store, she earned a reputation as a brilliant raconteur.

A literary celebrity within months of her arrival, Hurston found herself cultivated and sought out by New York's artistic community. She met such eminent black writers as Fauset, Arna Bontemps, Eric Walrond, and Bruce Nugent. She was also befriended by many of the city's sophisticated white writers, artists, and patrons of the arts. Popular novelist Fannie Hurst, humorist Irvin S. Cobb, and movie mogul Jesse Lasky were among the wealthy whites who invited her to dinner parties and nightclubs.

The Florida country girl was having the time of her life in the big city. Writing to a relative in Florida, she said, "I won't try to pretend that I'm not thrilled at the chance to see and do what I am. I love it.... I am just running wild in every direction, trying to see everything at once."

Among the things Hurston saw during her first year in New York were Fannie Hurst's elegant duplex apartment and Barnard College. Hurst, one of the judges of the *Opportunity* contest, had been impressed by Hurston's wit and obvious intelligence as well as by her writing talent. She invited Hurston to become her live-in secretary, a job the writer quickly accepted. Mystified by filing, unable to type or take shorthand, Hurston proved a disaster as a secretary, but she and Hurst became good friends.

Hurston continued to live with the novelist, acting as her chauffeur, companion, and, she hinted to friends, as Hurst's prize pet. The Negro, it was often said, was "in vogue," and Zora Neale Hurston always attracted attention. As the black novelist and physician Rudolph Fisher remarked in a 1927 magazine article, "Negro stock is going up and everybody's buying."

The *Opportunity* banquet had brought Hurston to the attention of another influential admirer: writer Annie Nathan Meyer, a founder of Barnard, the undergraduate college for women of Columbia University. Meyer, who also saw a brilliant mind beneath Hurston's

Gathered at an uptown branch of the New York Public Library, Harlem Renaissance members prepare for a literary club meeting. The tremendous upsurge in black artistic production

*during the 1920s generated both black pride and white curiosity.
"Negro stock is up and everybody's buying," quipped one black
novelist in 1927.*

flashy exterior and earthy wit, obtained a Barnard scholarship for the Florida writer; Zora began classes at the school in the fall of 1925.

Meanwhile, she continued to make waves among the Harlem literary set and took on the role of the "New Negro." The term had first emerged after World War I, when black leaders called on their followers to demand their rights. "The New Negro," stated one black publication in 1920, "realizes that there cannot be any qualified equality.... [The New Negro] is the product of the same world-wide forces that have brought into being the great liberal and radical movements that are now seizing the reins of political, economic and social power in all of the civilized countries of the world."

By the mid-1920s, "New Negro" had come to refer to members of Harlem's burgeoning literary movement. "The New Negro writers," observed historian Jervis Anderson in his 1981 book, *This Was Harlem: 1900–1950*, "could be said to represent in art what the race militants had represented in politics—not an appeal to compassion and social redress but a bold assertion of self."

Although she now bore the weighty label of "New Negro," Hurston never seemed to take herself—or anyone else—very seriously. "She had a great scorn for all pretensions," said Langston Hughes. Hurston often poked fun at people she considered pompous. To her, the sometimes solemn reformers of the NAACP were "Negrotarians"; even more outrageous to some observers was her cheerfully irreverent term for the group of young black literati to which she herself belonged: she called them "the niggerati."

Hurston's associates sometimes defended themselves with wicked satire. Writer Wallace Thurman, for example, aimed a telling barb at his friend and frequent sparring partner in his novel, *Infants of the Spring*. Thinly disguising Hurston as a character named Sweetie May Car, Thurman described her as "a short story writer, more noted for her ribald wit and personal effervescence than for any actual literary work."

Thurman's Sweetie May is in the habit of making light-hearted but cynical remarks: "Being a Negro writer these days is a racket and I'm going to make the most out of it while it lasts," she says at one point. "I don't know a tinker's damn about art. I care less about it.... About twice a year I manage to sell a story. It is acclaimed. I am a genius in the making. Thank God for this Negro literary renaissance! Long may it flourish!"

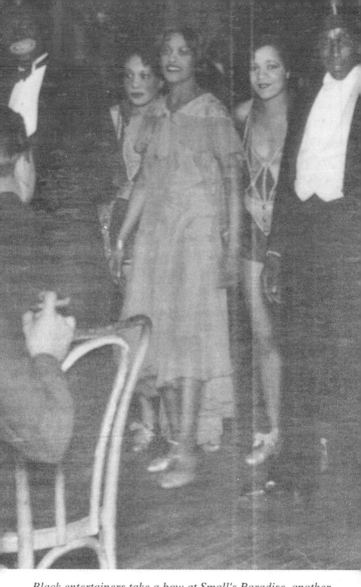

Black entertainers take a bow at Small's Paradise, another popular Harlem showplace of the 1920s. The Cotton Club barred African Americans as customers (but not as

entertainers!). However, Small's Paradise—which featured roller-skating waiters and astronomical prices—welcomed the money of all races.

"The Harlem Renaissance," observed Hemenway in his Hurston biography, "was not a white fad, but an indigenous spiritual revolution." Nevertheless, the wide extent of white interest and support—and the necessity of responding to it—created tensions among the black men and women of the Renaissance.

Some of Hurston's contemporaries considered her behavior devious, calculated to win sympathy and financial support from the Renaissance's white patrons. "She was always getting scholarships and things from wealthy white people," Langston Hughes once said, "some of whom simply paid her just to sit around and represent the Negro race for them, she did it in such a racy fashion."

Born and bred in the rural South, Hurston sometimes spoke with an earthiness that shocked her associates, many of them blacks with middle-class sensibilities. These were people who not only wanted to celebrate their own blackness but to elevate society's view of their race. They accused her of advancing her career by using "darky" talk and telling stories that reinforced the stereotypes by which whites had long mocked blacks.

Hurston certainly recognized the drawing power of her sharp ear for dialect and her gift for mimicry. And she certainly wanted to advance her career, sometimes using outrageous flattery to achieve her goals. But she was also being herself when she told the tales of her childhood. Her critics did not understand that she could not be expected, as Hemenway put it, "to repudiate the folk origins that were such a rich part of her total identity."

"Spunk," Hurston's second published short story, appeared in the June 1925 issue of *Opportunity*. More ambitious but perhaps less successful than the earlier "Drenched in Light," this story also takes place in an Eatonville-like setting. A tale of adultery and supernatural revenge, "Spunk" unfolds against a keenly observed backdrop of black southern life. The story was reprinted in *The New Negro*, a 1925 book edited by Hurston's former Howard University teacher Alain Locke. A mixture of essays, fiction and poetry, *The New Negro* met with immediate and widespread acclaim, quickly becoming the "Bible" of the Harlem Renaissance.

In his title essay for the book, Locke boldly called for a new black aesthetic. Along with Charles S. Johnson of *Opportunity* and James Weldon Johnson of the NAACP, Locke believed that art—literature especially—was the weapon that could pierce the racist armor of white America. "Nothing will do more to change the mental attitude and raise his status," wrote James Weldon Johnson, "than a demonstration of intellectual parity by the Negro through the production of literature and art."

W.E.B. Du Bois did not agree. "After all," he demanded, "what have we who are slaves and black to do with art?" Du Bois believed that black artists, as members of the Talented Tenth, had a twofold obligation: to educate blacks in their own cultural traditions, and to educate whites out of their cultural prejudices. No believer in "art for art's sake," Du Bois found the beauty of a work of art largely irrelevant if it was not politically useful.

For the group of young writers Hurston had named the "niggerati," the differences between Locke and Du Bois were more apparent than real. For these writers, whether or not their work had any propaganda value was immaterial. They also shied away from the cultural conservatism of such writers as Johnson and Locke. Hurston and her allies believed that while these men paid lip service to the richness of black heritage, they balked at publishing anything that seemed *too* rich, worried about reinforcing white stereotypes—and frightening away white financial support. The "niggerati" were determined to create art rooted in the life

Pianist Duke Ellington and his band appear at Harlem's legendary night spot, the Cotton Club. Specializing in smooth jazz, he was a favorite of the club's whites.

actually lived by ordinary black people.

Out of this determination, they created *Fire!!*, a magazine that appeared in November 1926. Its title taken from a Langston Hughes poem, *Fire!!* was intended to shock the sensibilities of the Renaissance. In this aim, it succeeded. Containing well-written stories on such "forbidden" subjects as child prostitution and homosexuality, *Fire!!* scandalized the very establishment on which its success depended.

Du Bois and Locke, among others, treated the magazine with patronizing disdain, overlooking the fact that its content was consistently superior to the writing that had appeared in *The New Negro*. Although it was a financial disaster, *Fire!!* was an unqualified artistic success.

Hurston's contributions to *Fire!!* consisted of a version of her *Opportunity* award-winning play, *Color Struck*, and a short story, "Sweat." The play, about color prejudice among blacks, is a minor if entertaining work, but "Sweat" is probably the finest piece of fiction that Hurston wrote during her association with the Harlem Renaissance.

The story is about Delia Jones, a deeply religious black woman who takes in white people's washing to support herself and her husband, Sykes. Humiliated by his wife's labor and

W.E.B. Du Bois, arguably the most powerful African-American voice of his time, believed that education—not art—was the key to black equality.

The distinguished painter of murals and portraits, Archibald Motley (shown here at a 1932 exhibition) first received recognition during the Harlem Renaissance.

Motley's "truly remarkable talent," observed the New York Times *in 1929, "has set the art-critical world to wondering and talking."*

his own inability to find work, Sykes treats Delia cruelly. He beats her, boasts about his good-looking mistress, and preys on her dread of snakes. All love for Sykes is long dead in Delia's heart; her only remaining pleasure is the local church, where she can find temporary respite from Sykes and her life of "sweat, sweat, sweat! Work and sweat, cry and sweat, pray and sweat!"

Characteristically, Hurston is concerned not only with presenting the relationship of Delia and Sykes but also with the townspeople's attitude toward their relationship. Delia and Sykes are part of a larger community, and their individual fates have a larger meaning within that community; indeed, part of the folkloric dimension of Hurston's work is just this awareness of the complex currents running back and forth between people and the cultural environments in which they live, each helping to determine the other.

Deciding to kill Delia, Sykes hides a rattlesnake in her washbasket, then goes off to get drunk. Delia escapes the snake by pure luck, and when the drunken Sykes returns, expecting to find her dead body, he is fatally bitten by the rattler himself. Delia, hiding outside the house, hears her husband "calling in a most despairing tone as one who expected no answer. The sun crept on up, and he called. Delia could not move—her legs had gone flabby. She never moved, he called, and the sun kept rising."

The dying Sykes, one eye swollen shut, crawls from the house. He sees Delia and realizes she has been there all along, listening to him die. He realizes, too, that she knows he tried to kill her and this is her revenge. Yet Sykes has his revenge as well, for by refusing to help or comfort her dying husband, Delia has assumed part of the guilt. Like Adam and Eve in the Garden of Eden, Delia and Sykes are bound together by shared sin. The tragic story demonstrates Hurston's skill at its best: "Sweat" shows, but does not judge.

Within a year of her arrival in New York, Hurston had become recognized as one of the most promising writers of the Harlem Renaissance.

Chapter Six

The Spy-glass
of Anthropology

WHEN ZORA HURSTON ENTERED
Barnard College in the fall of 1925, she was the
school's only black student. But, she reported
in her autobiography, "I have no lurid tales to
tell of race discrimination at Barnard." In fact,
she added cheerfully, "The Social Register
crowd soon took me up, and I became
Barnard's sacred black cow. If you had not had
lunch with me you had not shot from taw."
("Taw" is the line from which players shoot at
marbles.)

"I had the same feeling at Barnard that I did
at Howard, only more so," Hurston continued.

---

*Flanked by his great-great grandchildren, Cudjo Lewis relaxes at
his Mobile, Alabama, home. Hurston's published report on the
old man earned high—but undeserved—praise.*

"I felt that I was highly privileged and [I] determined to make the most of it. I did not resolve to be a grind, however, to show the white folks that I had brains. I took it for granted that they knew that."

Formally stating her interests as a freshman, Hurston wrote, with somewhat uncharacteristic modesty: "I have had some small success as a writer and wish above all to succeed at it." That intention changed over the following months, partly because Hurston was becoming disenchanted with the Harlem Renaissance scene, but mainly because of the influence of Dr. Franz Boas.

Because her academic program was "top-heavy" with English courses, Hurston recalled, her adviser suggested that she add a few other subjects, such as anthropology. A class in that subject introduced her to Boas, a Columbia University professor of anthropology and the author of such ground-breaking books as *The Mind of Primitive Man* (1911) and *Anthropology and Modern Man* (1928). Hurston came to idolize the elderly German-born scholar, whom she called "the king of kings."

Anthropology is the science of man and culture. It is divided into two major disciplines: physical anthropology, which is concerned with man as a biological organism; and cultural anthropology, which studies the customs, social relationships, and belief systems of mankind and its various racial, ethnic, cultural, and geographic subgroups.

In the 1920s, much anthropological research focused on the world's so-called "primitive" cultures. To most anthropologists, "primitive" referred not only to preliterate or preindustrial cultures, but to the cultures of nonwhite and non-European populations. African-American and Native-American cultures, for example, were considered primitive. This ethnocentric bias on the part of white anthropologists persisted for many years, clouding both the research of the scientists and the conclusions drawn from that research.

Franz Boas worked against this trend, believing that all races shared the same potential. Recognizing Hurston as an exceptionally gifted woman with a highly unusual background—for a Barnard student—he encouraged her to become a cultural anthropologist. He believed she should specialize in African-American folklore, studying the dances, songs, stories, jokes, and folk medicine of the southern black community in which she had been raised.

Boas and other anthropologists thought of

folklore as the spontaneous, collective expression of a people's spirit, as whatever it was that made them what they were. Hurston defined folklore as "the art people create before they find out there is such a thing as art."

She decided that the study of folklore could give her something that writing fiction could not provide: the distance she needed to come to terms with her Eatonville heritage. In *Mules and Men*, her 1935 book on black culture, she said that, in one sense, studying folklore would not be a new experience for her.

"When I pitched headforemost into the world I landed in the crib of negroism," Hurston wrote. "From the earliest rocking of my cradle, I had known about the capers Brer Rabbit is apt to cut and what the Squinch Owl says from the house top. But it was fitting me like a tight chemise [undergarment]. I couldn't see it for wearing it. It was only when I was off in college, away from my native surroundings, that I could see myself like somebody else and stand off and look at my garment. Then I had to have the spy-glass of anthropology to look through at that."

By February 1927, Hurston had completed most of her Barnard course work; she was ready to take the methods she had learned in the classroom into the field. Boas obtained a

Hurston adored Franz Boas, the eminent anthropologist who became her teacher and friend at Barnard College. He also obtained a $1400 scholarship for her.

$1,400 scholarship for her from the Association for the Study of Negro Life and History; the money would allow her to make a six-month collecting trip from Jacksonville to New Orleans, sponsored by Columbia's anthropology department. Her assignment was simply to record as much African-American folklore as she could find.

Both Hurston and Boas were excited about the trip. It would be the first time that a black folklorist with Hurston's unique blend of training and background would attempt such a task. Boas was convinced that Hurston, a black woman with deep roots in the rural South, would be able to gain the trust of her informants in a way that no white or northern black collector could ever hope to do. Most of the African-American folklore compiled to date had been collected by whites who had preconceived notions of black culture and who altered the material, consciously or unconsciously, to reflect their own prejudices.

Hurston agreed that she would have a better chance of gathering black folklore than a white researcher. "You see," she explained in her autobiography, "We [blacks] are a polite people and we do not say to our questioner, 'Get out of here!'... The theory behind our tactics: 'The white man is always trying to know into somebody else's business. All right, I'll set something outside the door of my mind for him to play with and handle. He can read my writing but he sho' can't read my mind. I'll put this play toy in his hand, and he will seize it and go away. Then I'll say my say and sing my song.'"

Full of confidence in her own abilities, Hurston boarded a Florida-bound train in late February 1927. When she got to Jacksonville, she bought a car, christened it "Sassie Susie," and set to work.

The work did not go well. Despite her training, this was Hurston's first real attempt to collect folklore, and she had not yet developed an effective approach. As she put it, "The glamour of Barnard College was still upon me. I dwelt in marble halls. I knew where the material was all right. But, I went about asking, in carefully accented Barnardese, 'Pardon me, but do you know any folk-tales or folk-songs?' The men and women who had whole treasuries of material just looked at me and shook their heads." Hurston did get "a few little items," she said. "But compared with what I did later, not enough to make a flea a waltzing jacket."

After three months of largely futile effort, Hurston took time off for a very special reason. She and Herbert Sheen, her Howard University sweetheart, had been informally engaged for the past six years; now they decided to take the big step. In May, Hurston drove to St. Augustine, Florida, and married Sheen.

Unfortunately, the marriage went no better than the folklore collecting. Almost as soon as the ceremony was over, Hurston decided she had made a mistake. "I had an uncomfortable feeling of unreality..., and I wondered why," she reported in her autobiography. "Who had canceled the well-advertised tour of the moon? Somebody had turned a hose on the sun. What I had taken for eternity turned out to be a moment walking in its sleep." (The couple were to go their separate ways the following August and, four years later, to obtain a friendly divorce.)

Hurston was expected to send the folklore she collected to the Association for the Study of Negro Life and History, which had underwritten her trip. The association's officials, who planned to publish Hurston's material in the *Journal of Negro History*, were particularly excited by an interview she had scheduled for July in Mobile, Alabama. Hurston would be talking to Cudjo Lewis, a black man who had been brought to America as a slave in 1859.

Lewis had been captured in Africa and transported to America on an illegal slave ship, the *Clotilde*. (The United States had banned the importation of slaves in 1807.) The last survivor of the *Clotilde*'s passengers, Lewis was nearly ninety years old in 1927, but he retained vivid memories of his African childhood. Hurston's expedition had so far produced little; her interview with this feisty old man promised an opportunity to end the trip in a blaze of glory.

Instead, the interview almost ruined Hurston's career. Her article on Lewis, "Cudjo's Own Story of the Last African Slaver," impressed many readers when it appeared in the October 1927 issue of the *Journal of Negro History*. In writing it, however, Hurston had committed a deadly academic sin: she plagiarized the work of another scholar. According to biographer Hemenway, Hurston wrote twenty-five percent of the piece and copied the rest from *Historic Sketches of the Old South*, a 1914 book she found at the Mobile Historical Society.

Did Hurston lift the material because she was frustrated by the difficulties she was encountering in her collecting? Was her act the result of pressures created by her already disintegrating marriage? We will probably never know, because Hurston never said a word about the subject.

Her plagiarism, in fact, remained undetected

The grant Franz Boas had managed to obtain for Hurston from the Columbia anthropology department enabled her to spend six months in Mobile (shown here in the 1920s), and New Orleans.

Her assignment was to record as much African-American folklore as possible. In New Orleans she became fascinated with the ancient African religion, voodoo.

until another scholar discovered it in 1972. But the knowledge that she had stolen from another writer must have added to Hurston's feelings of failure about her first collecting trip. In her autobiography, she said she returned to New York in August "with my heart beneath my knees and my knees in some lonesome valley."

Hemenway theorizes that Hurston's plagiarism was meant to be discovered, that it was an unconscious attempt at "academic suicide." Hurston cherished the culture of her people, but she had always used it as a springboard for her own poetic interpretations. To approach that culture with an attitude of scientific detachment must have seemed not only boring but somehow dishonest to Hurston at the beginning of her career as a folklorist.

Hurston was discovering that the "spy-glass of anthropology" had its drawbacks: for that instrument to be effective, its user must stand away from the object of scrutiny. Hurston had wanted to reexamine her past from a distance, but not, perhaps, from quite such a long distance as science required.

Another element in the plagiarism puzzle is Hurston's perception of folklore. In a town like Eatonville, where storytelling assumes a ritual importance, the stories are no one's private property. Anyone is free to tell them, to change them, to borrow something from one version and something else from another, to create a third version from which another person will borrow in turn. Folklore evolves by a collective, communal process. In her own work, Hurston consistently blurred the divisions between folklore and fiction, between objective scientist and creative artist. Although she was undoubtedly aware of her serious mistake in plagiarizing the work of another, she may have seen the act as not so different, really, from what she had been doing all her life, from what she had learned to do on the porch of Joe Clarke's store.

Preparing to leave Mobile after her interview with Cudjo Lewis, Hurston ran into her friend Langston Hughes. On a tour of the South, Hughes had been giving poetry readings and getting to know a culture he had, for the most part, only read about in books. Hurston and Hughes decided to drive back to New York together. Herbert Sheen, Hurston's husband of two months, was already on his way back to medical school in Chicago.

"I knew it would be fun traveling with her," Hughes recalled later. "It was." On the long drive north in Sassie Susie, Hurston and Hughes cemented their friendship, sharing money and food, exchanging choice bits of folklore collected over the summer, and discussing a plan to collaborate on a folk opera.

Hughes also talked to Hurston about an exciting new acquaintance: an elderly, eccentric and extremely rich white woman he had recently met through Alain Locke. Her name was Charlotte van der Veer Quick Mason, but Hughes was already calling her by the name she preferred: Godmother. Almost fanatically dedicated to African-American art and artists, "Godmother" Mason was to have an extraordinary effect on the lives of both Hughes and Hurston.

A portrait of Langston Hughes painted by his patron, Amy Spingarn. For a while Hughes and Hurston were friends but fell out after their adaptation of Hurston's Mules and Men *into a play called* Mule Bone. *Hurston had Hughes' name deleted from the credits of the play, insisting that she had rewritten their work, and the play that was produced was entirely her own effort.*

Chapter Seven

Inside of Negro Art and Lore

As SOON AS HE and Zora Hurston reached New York in early September 1927, Langston Hughes paid a call on his patron, the immensely wealthy Charlotte Mason. Intrigued by the young poet's report on his traveling companion, Mason invited Hurston to tea at her sumptuous Park Avenue apartment.

An amateur anthropologist, Mason was deeply fascinated—perhaps even obsessed— by "primitive" cultures, which she felt possessed a vigor absent from the effete and rapidly decaying civilization of the white

St. Louis Cathedral. A devout Catholic, the New Orleans Voodoo Queen Marie Laveau worshipped here nearly every day of her life, even after she gained fame as a voodoo priestess.

race. The elderly woman was also an enthusiastic supporter of contemporary black literature and painting. By the time Hurston met her, Mason had already contributed more than $50,000—a tremendous sum in the 1920s—to the writers and artists of the Harlem Renaissance.

Apparently, Mason genuinely liked the black writers and scholars with whom she surrounded herself. Still, she made it more than clear just who was in charge: insisting that her visiting protegees call her "Godmother," she seated them on footstools arranged in a circle around her own high, throne-like chair. She listened in rapt silence when her visitors discussed art or poetry or religion, but if she detected a note of insincerity, she would thunder: "That is nothing! It has no soul in it. You have broken the law!"

Describing Mason in her autobiography, Hurston said, "Her tongue was a knout [whip], cutting off your outer pretenses, and bleeding your vanity like a rusty nail. She was merciless to a lie, spoken, acted or insinuated." Nevertheless, Hurston took an immediate liking to the formidable old woman. She also assumed, correctly, that Mason might help her develop her career as a folklorist.

At their first meeting, Hurston turned on

the charm, treating Mason to the full Eatonville repertoire. "I must tell the tales, sing the songs, do the dances, and repeat the raucous sayings and doings of the Negro furthest down," reported Hurston. "[Mason] is altogether in sympathy with them, because she says truthfully they are utterly sincere in living."

Hurston's irony here is unmistakable: there is nothing like a little poverty and oppression to make for real sincerity. Mason saw Hurston, says Robert Hemenway, as "an unspoiled child of nature," and Hurston played the role to the hilt. She may have resented Mason's demands, but she seems to have truly respected her. "My relations with Godmother were curious," she wrote later. "Laugh if you will, but there was and is a psychic bond between us. She could read my mind, [and I] could read her thoughts."

Much impressed by Hurston's accounts of her own work, Mason offered to subsidize her. In December 1927, the two women signed a contract: Mason would supply Hurston with a car and pay her a monthly salary of $200 for a year's worth of folklore collecting in the South. In return, Hurston had to give up control of her material: whatever data she acquired on the trip would belong to Mason.

Sent south to study southern folklore, Hurston spent time in Mobile, then traveled to Polk County, Florida, and to a deep-woods community of lumber camp workers, who lived in housing

such as shown here. The camp promised a rich source of folk songs, dances, stories, and jokes; but it also, as Hurston was soon to learn, promised danger from the hard-drinking workers.

Hurston was also prohibited from publishing anything without Mason's permission during the period of the contract. Langston Hughes had entered on a similar contract the previous month, but his support had fewer strings attached.

Hurston signed the contract cheerfully, aware that she had limited options. She lacked the academic credentials to apply for a research grant, and she was not even scheduled to graduate from Barnard for another year. Charlotte Mason was the nearest thing to a fairy godmother she could hope for.

On December 14, Hurston left New York for Mobile, Alabama. She would spend the next sixteen months immersed in the folk culture of the black South, not just observing it as an impartial scientist but participating in it as well.

"My search for knowledge of things took me into many strange places and adventures," Hurston noted. "My life was in danger several times. If I had not learned how to take care of myself in these circumstances, I could have been maimed or killed on most any day of my research work."

The dangers—and rewards—of Hurston's work were demonstrated at a lumber camp in Polk County, Florida. The camp promised a rich source of folk songs, dances, stories, and jokes; populated by hard-bitten, hard-drinking women and men, it also promised trouble. By befriending the camp's toughest woman, Big Sweet, Hurston provided herself with two valuable assets: an informed source and a protector.

Through Big Sweet, Hurston was accepted into the community. But she also made enemies. After spending several weeks in the camp, she started collecting songs from a guitar picker named Slim. "He was a valuable source of material to me," Hurston recalled, "so I built him up a bit by buying him drinks and letting him ride in my car." This was too much for Slim's former girlfriend, Lucy. Hurston, announced Lucy, had stolen her man and needed killing.

One night in the camp tavern, Hurston glanced at the door and froze. Lucy, knife in hand, was heading straight for her. "I saw sudden death very near that moment," Hurston wrote later. Big Sweet charged Lucy and disarmed her, starting a full-scale battle. "Switch-blades, ice-picks and old-fashioned razors were out," said Hurston. "Big Sweet yelled for me to run. I really ran, too. I ran out of the place, ran to my room, threw my things in the car and left the place. When the

Upon arriving in New Orleans to pursue her interest in voodoo, Hurston moved into a rooming house on St. Ann Street (the three-story building at right. It is now a guest house for tourists.

No doubt Hurston knew she'd rented a room directly across the street from this house (now the "Marie Laveau" apartments). For the last decades of her life, Marie Laveau's home stood here.

sun came up I was a hundred miles up the road, headed for New Orleans."

Such narrow escapes did nothing to dampen Hurston's enthusiasm, but after her experience in Polk County, she started carrying a revolver on her trips.

On her way to New Orleans, Hurston wrote a letter to Hughes, telling him about the events in Polk County and about how exciting her work had become. "I am getting inside of Negro art and lore," she said. "Most gorgeous possibilities are showing themselves constantly." In an essay written several years later, she observed, "Negro folklore is not a thing of the past. It is still in the making. Its great variety shows the adaptability of the black man: nothing is too old or too new, domestic or foreign, high or low, for his use."

In New Orleans, Hurston embarked on a major investigation of "hoodoo," a form of magic that probably originated in Africa. Belief in hoodoo was widespread among rural southern blacks, as well as among many whites in southern Louisiana. Hoodoo, according to its believers, can accomplish many things: it can heal sickness, improve love affairs, bring fortune in business dealings, remove curses, get rid of ghosts, and bring bad luck or even death to enemies.

"Nobody knows for sure how many thousands in America are warmed by the fire of hoodoo, because the worship is bound in secrecy," Hurston wrote in *Mules and Men*. "It is not the accepted theology of the Nation and so believers conceal their faith.... Nobody can say where it begins or ends. Mouths don't empty themselves unless the ears are sympathetic and knowing."

Determined to learn everything she could about this ancient faith, Hurston studied under the Frizzly Rooster and four other "power doctors," undergoing an initiation ceremony with each. After much "stumbling" and many false leads, she managed to meet Luke Turner, the leading hoodoo practitioner of New Orleans. Although highly suspicious of Hurston at first, Turner finally agreed to endow her with the "crown of power," a mystical degree that allowed its wearer to commune with the spirits.

The endowment ceremony, said Hurston, "was not only elaborate, it was impressive." For three days and nights, she lay naked on a couch that had been covered by a rattlesnake skin. She was allowed no food during this period, but a pitcher of water was placed near her head—"so my soul," she explained, "would not wander off in search of water and

When Hurston was studying in New Orleans, this park on
Rampart Street was still called "Congo Square," as it was in
the time of Marie Laveau, who held Sunday afternoon voodoo

ceremonies there. More profane ceremonies were held in the swamps of St. John's Bayou, several miles back of town. The park name was changed to honor Louis Armstrong.

be attacked by evil influences and not return to me." During this period, Hurston reported, she dreamed "strange exalted dreams." In one, she said, "I strode across the heavens with lightning flashing from under my feet, and grumbling thunder following in my wake."

Hurston's reports on her experiences with hoodoo and other forms of magic contain a double note: although she approaches the subject with scientific detachment, she implies that hoodoo, at least sometimes, actually works. "I hold that any religion that satisfies the individual urge is valid for that person," she once commented. And concluding an explanation of hoodoo in *Mules and Men*, she writes, "That's what the old ones said in ancient times and we talk it again." Hurston's readers are left to decide for themselves if the author regards hoodoo as mere superstition or as genuine magic.

From New Orleans, where she stayed until the spring of 1929, Hurston returned to Florida. Mason had renewed her contact for another year, which gave her the freedom to do a bit of further exploring. After putting her field notes in order and doing some further collecting in and around Miami, she spent a few weeks in Nassau, the Bahamas. There, she became fascinated by the local blacks' songs, which she described as "more original, dynamic and African than American Negro songs." In the Bahamas, she observed with delight, "nothing is too big, or little, to be 'put in sing.'"

Returning to Miami in October, Hurston sent her material to Mason, who was to oversee its publication. Mason and Alain Locke, who sometimes acted as her assistant, agreed that Hurston had collected enough folktales for a book, already titled by Hurston *Mules and Men*. But her material, they said, required some organizing and polishing before it could go to the printer. Mason also told Hurston she would have to do a bit of pruning. In a letter to Hughes, Hurston reported, "Godmother says the dirty words must be toned down. Of course, I knew that, but first I wanted to collect them as they are."

In February 1930, Hurston headed north, settling in Westfield, New Jersey. Mason had selected Westfield, safely removed from the distractions of New York City, as a suitable place for both Hurston and Hughes to work. Installing the writers in modest rooming houses, the Godmother paid their rent and hired a literary secretary, Louise Thompson, to assist them. Thompson, a University of

A "voodoo doll." Now sold to tourists, these were used by the followers of voodoo, which, in New Orleans was refined into a mixture of *Voodoo* and *Catholicism* by Marie Laveau.

St. Louis Cemetery #1 tomb of "Madame de Paris," the original Marie Laveau. A century later, believers still leave flowers, as they also do at the "Marie Laveau" tomb of her daughter!

California graduate and former Hampton Institute teacher, had known Hughes since 1928, when she was briefly married to his longtime friend, novelist Wallace Thurman. While Hurston set to work revising *Mules and Men*, Hughes checked the proofs of his first novel, *Not Without Laughter.*

Delighted to be reunited and eager to make up for lost time, Hurston and Hughes soon began to plan the folk opera they had discussed for so long. Then, after some discussion, they decided to write a comedy instead, based on a folktale Hurston had collected. Hurston and Hughes wanted to create "the first real Negro folk comedy," a play whose authenticity would stand in sharp contrast to the stereotypical portrayals of black character and culture in the era's popular dramas.

The story of *Mule Bone*, as the authors titled their play, revolves around a romantic triangle in a small, Eatonville-like town. Competing for the hand of a pretty young woman, two friends, Jim and Dave, come to blows. But when the young men realize that the object of their affections expects them to serve the white folks, as she does, they give her up and resume their old friendship.

Hughes gave the play its dramatic shape, Hurston supplied the central idea and authentic southern dialogue, and Thompson typed the result. Although the trio often laughed helplessly together, particuarly when Hurston acted out parts of the play, all was not harmony. Although Hurston had never been romantically involved with Hughes, she began to appear jealous of his friendship—also strictly nonromantic—with Thompson. For whatever reason (she never alluded to the subject in writing), Hurston left Westfield in May, promising to complete the play's unfinished second act during the summer.

At the end of May, the eccentric and domineering Mason, infuriated because Hughes had gone to Washington without her permission, severed her relationship with him. Not long afterward, Mason also dismissed Thompson, calling her—and most other blacks—a "lost cause." Thompson took the astonishing announcement philosophically, but Hughes was devastated. Beset by various illnesses, he went to stay with his mother in Cleveland, Ohio. There, in January 1931, he received even more distressing news.

Hughes learned that a Cleveland group of black actors, the Gilpin Players, were preparing to stage a new folk comedy. Its title: *Mule Bone*; its author: Zora Neale Hurston. The second act was new, and the first and third acts had been revised, but this was the same *Mule Bone* that Hughes and Hurston had worked on in Westfield.

Hughes telephoned Hurston and demanded an explanation. She told him she had no idea how the play had gotten to Cleveland. (As it happened, one of Hurston's New York literary friends, to whom she had given a copy, had sent the play to Cleveland without Hurston's knowledge or consent.) Nevertheless, Hurston's name appeared on the play and Hughes' did not.

Hurston then wrote Hughes a letter, asserting that the play was all hers. "It was my story from beginning to end," she said. "It was my dialogue, my situations." Conceding that most of the play was indeed Hurston's work, Hughes offered her two-thirds of the royalties if she would agree to a joint byline. Hurston refused to budge; the play, she insisted, was hers alone.

Which of these two talented, sensitive people wrote what parts of *Mule Bone* will most likely never be known. The play, which marked the end of Hurston's and Hughes' long friendship, was never performed during their lifetimes; unlike the feuding characters in *Mule Bone*, Hurston and Hughes were never reconciled.

A few months after the Cleveland quarrel, in March 1931, Godmother Mason released Hurston from her contract. Although she would continue to receive occasional checks from Mason, Hurston was now a free agent for the first time in three years.

Convinced, despite the *Mule Bone* fiasco, that folklore had great theatrical potential, Hurston decided to create a Broadway show. In mid-1931, she put together some of the work songs, children's game songs, blues, and spirituals she had collected and wove them into a review called *The Great Day.* "LET THE PEOPLE SING, was and is my motto," said Hurston in her autobiography.

In order to pay for costumes, theater rental, publicity, and the fifty-two singers and dancers she engaged, Hurston pawned her radio and sold the car Mason had given her. Still far short of funds, she appealed to Mason for a loan; Godmother obliged with enough money to stage the show for one night—January 10, 1932—at New York's John Golden Theater.

"Because I know that music without motion is not natural with my people," Hurston wrote later, "I did not have the singers stand in a stiff group and reach for the high note. I told them to just imagine that they were in [a Baptist church] and go ahead." Her instructions worked. *The Great Day*, which recreated twenty-four hours in the life of a group of railroad-camp workers, played to a full house of wildly applauding patrons and received glowing reviews in the newspapers. Although net profits came to only $261—not enough to pay back Mason's $530 loan—Hurston was delighted. "The world wanted to hear the glorious voice of my people," she said happily.

A few months after her Broadway success, Hurston decided to return to Eatonville, where she hoped to finish her work on *Mules and Men* in relative tranquility. "Back in my native village," she recalled later, "I edited the huge mass of material I had, arranged it [in] some sequence and laid it aside."

Although finally completed, *Mules and Men* was not to see publication until 1935. By that time, folklorist Hurston would have turned into novelist Hurston. Her new foray into the realm of fiction was to begin in the world where she had started.

Zora Neale Hurston at about the time she was in New Orleans. She was married for two months, but soon her husband was on his way back to medical school.

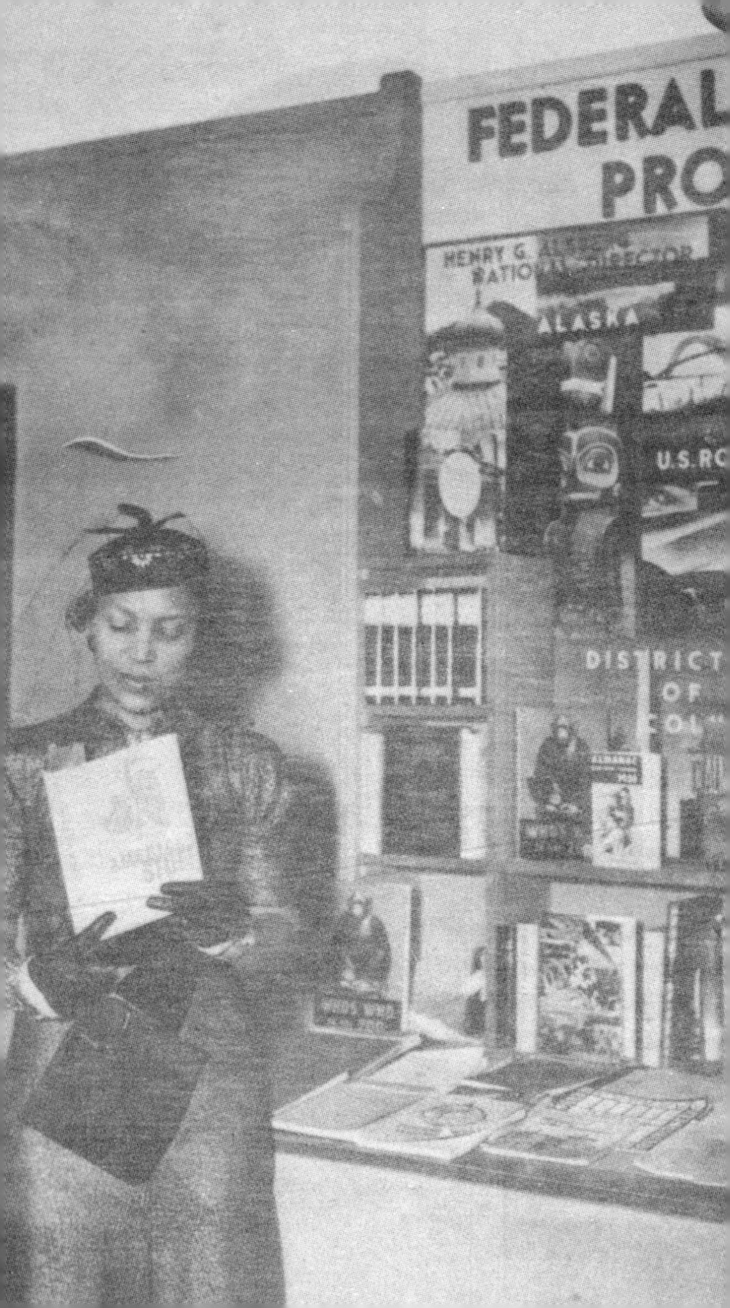
FEDERAL
PRO
ALASKA
U.S. RO
DISTRICT
OF

Chapter Eight

Success and Controversy

Zora HURSTON REENTERED the world of fiction with a masterful short story, "The Gilded Six-Bits." Completed in early 1933 and set in her semifictional Eatonville, the story weaves a tale of love and infidelity very different from such predecessors as "Spunk" and "Sweat." These earlier stories deal with betrayal and revenge; "The Gilded Six-Bits" is about betrayal and forgiveness. Less dependent on folklore, the story nonetheless shows Hurston's continued interest in the life of "the Negro furthest down."

One of Hurston's friends, a college English

Hurston checks out the Federal Writers' Project booth at a mid-1930s Manhattan book fair. The project aided such writers as Hurston, Ralph Ellison, and Richard Wright.

professor, was so impressed with the piece that he sent it to *Story* magazine. To Hurston's delight, *Story*, a prestigious journal that specialized in high-quality short fiction, published her tale in its August 1933 issue. To her further delight, "The Gilded Six-Bits" brought her a letter from book publisher Bertram Lippincott. Had Hurston, inquired Lippincott, written any fiction of book length? The author cheerfully replied that she was indeed at work on a novel—although, she later confessed in her autobiography, "not the first word was on paper when I wrote him that letter."

Hurston had, however, been *thinking* about a novel for the past several years. The idea for the book had come to her in 1929, but she had put it aside. Lippincott's question was the encouragement she needed to pick it up again. A week after she got the publisher's letter, she moved from Eatonville to nearby Sanford; there, she said, "I was not so much at home as at Eatonville, and could concentrate more and sat down to write *Jonah's Gourd Vine*."

In Sanford, Hurston rented a one-room house for $1.50 a week. Living on fifty cents loaned to her each week by a sympathetic cousin, she finished the novel in three months, then enlisted one friend to type the manuscript and another to pay for its postage to New York

City. Hopeful, nervous—and totally broke—she sat back and waited for news.

It came two weeks later, on the morning of October 16, 1933, but it was not the news she had hoped for: her landlady announced she was evicting Hurston for nonpayment of rent. The beleaguered writer promised she would pay the eighteen dollars in back rent soon, but the landlady refused to budge. "She said," Hurston recalled later, "she didn't believe that I would ever have that much money."

A few hours after that conversation, Hurston received a telegram with news of an entirely different order: Lippincott wanted her book and offered an advance of $200. "I never expect to have a greater thrill than that wire gave me," she recalled jublilantly.

Lippincott published *Jonah's Gourd Vine* in May 1934. The novel tells the story of John and Lucy Pearson—characters who share much of the history, as well as the first names, of Hurston's parents. Eatonville is again the setting. Like John Hurston, John Pearson is frequently unfaithful to his wife; plagued with guilt about his acts, he accuses her of spiteful nagging, even as she lies on her deathbed. "Ah do ez Ah please. You jus' uh hold back tuh me nohow," he snaps at her. "Big talk ain't changin' what you doin'," she replies. "You can't clean yo self wid yo tongue lak a cat." In response, her husband, who has never before raised his hand against her, strikes the dying woman. From this point on, John Pearson's life spins downward toward his own death.

This shocking scene, Hurston once explained, gave the novel its title. "You see," she said, "the prophet of God [Jonah] sat up under a gourd vine [symbolizing Pearson's success and relative prosperity] that had grown up in one night. But a worm [Pearson's pride, guilt, and violent temper] came along and cut it down. Great and sudden growth. One act of malice and it is withered and gone."

Pearson is a powerful figure; when he preaches, he is mightily caught up in the spirit of God, and when he strikes his wife, he is similarly caught up in a dark force beyond his understanding or control. Pearson's way of dealing with problems is to run from them; he never learns that he is really running from himself, a pattern that leads to his death.

Hurston believed that many blacks had been instilled with a sense of powerlessness as the result of slavery and the implacable racism that succeeded it. John Pearson's tragedy, as Hurston viewed it, is not just that of an individual man; it is the tragedy of the black man in America.

But *Jonah's Gourd Vine* is also a story of celebration. Hurston's travels throughout the South had made her more sure than ever that the black race's artistic genius had improved upon the white cultural forms forced upon it. "While [the Negro] lives in the midst of a white civilization, everything that he touches is reinterpreted for his own use," she observed. Chief among these reinterpreted forms was Christianity. "The prayer of the white man is considered humorous," Hurston wrote. "The beauty of the Old Testament does not exceed that of a Negro prayer." And it is there that John Pearson's brilliance shines brightest.

Not even slavery, asserted Hurston, had been able to separate her people from their heritage. In one of the sermons she wrote for John Pearson, he speaks in the voice of a slave. "'I, who am borne away to become an orphan, carry my parents with me,'" he says. "'For *Rhythm* is she not my mother and Drama is her man?' So he groaned aloud in the ships and hid his drum and laughed."

A Book-of-the-Month Club selection, *Jonah's Gourd Vine* received uniformly high praise from the nation's book reviewers. Hurston found their words exhilarating but also strangely disappointing. The critics, all of them white, saw her characters as colorful, fascinating, but alien beings. One reviewer, in fact, described them as "part and parcel of their race, which is as different from ours as night and day." Another critic said the novel's events were "described with a delicacy not often encountered in negro fiction." Still another headlined his favorable review "Darktown Strutter."

The *New York Times* found only one fault with the book: Pearson's fieriest sermon, said the newspaper, was "too good, too brilliantly splashed with poetic imagery to be the product of any one Negro preacher." Writing to her friend James Weldon Johnson about the *Times* reviewer, Hurston said, "He means well, I guess, but I never saw such a lack of information about us. It just seems that he is unwilling to believe that a Negro preacher could have so much poetry in him. When you and I...know that there are hundreds of preachers who are equalling that sermon weekly. He does not know that merely being a good man is not enough to hold a Negro preacher in an important charge. He must also be an artist. He must be both a poet and an actor of a very high order."

As an artist herself, Hurston also practiced several disciplines. She had always believed that black American culture deserved to be demonstrated not only by the written word but visually and aurally as well. "My people," she said, "are not going to do but so much of anything before they sing something."

Ever since producing her stunning show, *The Great Day*, in 1932, Hurston had searched for opportunities to repeat and enlarge it. In 1933, she presented a similar musical drama, *From Sun to Sun*, in several Florida towns; in 1934, she took the show, this time called *Singing Steel*, to St. Louis and Chicago. The presentations were greeted with enthusiasm by white viewers, but a number of middle-class blacks criticized them as demeaning to a people still struggling for respect in a white world. Blacks, these critics said, should discard such "primitive" displays, seeking instead to follow the traditions of white society.

This argument enraged Hurston. "Who knows," she demanded in a 1934 newspaper article, "what fabulous cities of artistic concepts lie within the mind and language of some humble Negro boy or girl who has never heard of [Norwegian playwright Henrik] Ibsen?" Lashing out at blacks who wanted to copy whites, she continued: "Fawn as you will. Spend an eternity standing awe struck. Roll your eyes in ecstasy and ape [the white man's] every move, but until we have placed something on his street corner that is our own, we are right back where we were when they filed our iron collar off."

Although Hurston fiercely defended black folkways and their important contibutions to American culture, she bristled at people who suggested that she concentrate on black politics in her work. "From what I had read and heard," she wrote in her autobiography, "Negroes were supposed to write about the Race Problem. I was and am thoroughly sick of the subject. My interest lies in what makes a man or a woman do such-and-so, regardless of his color. It seemed to me that the human beings I met reacted pretty much the same to the same stimuli. Different idioms, yes. Inherent difference, no."

The success of *Jonah's Gourd Vine* led to another contract with Lippincott: *Mules and Men* would appear at last. Published in October 1935, the book drew enthusiastic praise in journals ranging from the *Saturday Review* to the *New York Times* to the *New Republic*. One critic recommended *Mules and Men* for its "black magic and dark laughter," and another said it would give (white) readers "a very fair idea of how the other color enjoys life." *Mules and Men*, wrote an NAACP official, "is more than a collection of folklore. It is a valuable picture of the life of the unsophisticated Negro in small towns and backwoods of Florida."

Indeed, *Mules and Men* presented a unique treasury of African-American folklore and hoodoo. In collecting her material for the book, Hurston had used the methodology of her scientific training but rejected its demand for total objectivity. "I needed my Barnard education to help me see my people as they really are," she explained in a newspaper interview. "But I found that it did not do to be too detached as I stepped aside to study them. I had to go back, dress as they did, talk as they did, live their life, so that I could get into my stories the world I knew as a child."

In other words, Hurston had chosen to do more than present a scholarly collection of folktales; she had filled gaps between the tales by portraying their tellers and the way they lived. In doing so, she made it seem as if the tales sprang from their natural environment. She managed this feat by creating semifictional settings based on her own experiences in collecting and then featuring herself as narrator. By putting herself at the center of the book, Hurston was also symbolically stating her dependence upon black culture: it surrounded her, propping her up "on ev'y leanin' side," as one of her characters might have put it.

Hurston heads upriver with a local guide in Jamaica. She spent six months there living with, and studying the culture of, the Maroons, descendants of escaped slaves.

Mules and Men generated critical questions that were to dog Hurston for the rest of her career. Some critics—most of them black intellectuals—complained that her rich, emotionally complex portrayal of Eatonville glossed over an essential portion of the black experience. Poet and critic Sterling Brown, for one, wrote that Hurston's depiction of black life failed to take into account the poverty, disease, violence, enforced ignorance, and exploitation that formed a part of black southern life. *Mules and Men*, he asserted, "should be more bitter; it would be nearer the total truth."

Brown spoke for a sizeable part of the intellectual black community. The Great Depression, which had gripped the land since the stock market crash of 1929, had provided a fresh excuse for racism. In this environment, said many black leaders, black writers should be creating a literature of protest, spotlighting the cruel and ugly ways in which blacks had been victimized by white oppression. Hurston's assertion that "the Negro story teller is lacking in bitterness" struck her critics as a blatant falsehood.

Hurston acknowledged the reality of oppression, but she detested the self-pity of what she called the "sobbing school of Negrohood." She preferred to accentuate the positive in the black experience, alluding only indirectly to the psychological and economic wounds of slavery and segregation. To Hurston, black culture was not a defensive response to white racism, but rather the free and joyful expression of a people's unique genius. "We talk about the race problem a great deal, but go on living and laughing and striving like everybody else," she said.

Eager to extend her knowledge of black life in the western hemisphere, Hurston decided to study folklore and voodoo in the West Indies. She applied for a Guggenheim fellowship to finance the trip; receiving it in the spring of 1935, she headed for Kingston, Jamaica.

Hurston stayed in Jamaica for six months, spending most of that time in the rugged St. Catharine Mountains. There, she lived with the Maroons, descendants of slaves who had fought their way to freedom centuries earlier. Asking few questions at first, she gradually earned the trust of this community, which she called "a seething Africa." The Maroons allowed her to go on a ceremonial wild boar hunt, taught her about their medicinal and poisonous herbs, and let her participate in "The Nine Night," a frenzied, nine-day funeral ritual designed to keep the "duppy," or walking dead, from reappearing to harm the living.

In September, Hurston traveled to Haiti. There she found an intricate brand of voodoo that was "both beautiful and terrifying"—one that made the conjuring ceremonies of Louisiana seem tame. "Voodoo in Haiti," wrote Hurston, "has gathered about itself more details of gods and rites than the Catholic church has in Rome." To the accompaniment of flickering torchlight and pounding drums, she witnessed animal sacrifices, trances, the drinking of fresh blood, and apparent miracles (as when, during one funeral rite, the corpse abruptly, Hurston said, "sat up with its staring eyes, bowed its head and fell back again").

In Haiti, Hurston found three classes of people: "There is the quick, the dead, and then there are Zombies." Zombies, she explained, "are the bodies without souls. The living dead." Fear of these creatures, she added, "seeps over the country like a ground current of cold air." Haiti's powerful rituals and beliefs had a profound effect on Hurston, who later reported that she had actually seen and touched a Zombie.

"I listened to the broken noises in its throat, and then," she said, "I did what no one else had ever done, I photographed it." Hurston's experience left her convinced. "I know there are Zombies in Haiti," she stated firmly. "People have been called back from the dead."

Excited as she was by Haiti, Hurston did more there than simply observe the people and their practices: she wrote her second novel. At the end of December 1936, she sent the book, *Their Eyes Were Watching God*, to her New York publisher. When she returned to the United States the following March, she learned that Lippincott had scheduled the novel for September publication.

Hurston had gone to the West Indies not only to study but to end a stormy love affair with a considerably younger man. "A.W.P.," as she calls the twenty-three-year-old divinity student in *Dust Tracks on a Road*, adored the forty-five-year-old Hurston, and she returned his love wholeheartedly. "He was tall, dark brown, magnificently built," she recalled, "but I did not fall in love with him just for that. He had a fine mind and that intrigued me.... It seems to me that God must have put in extra time making him up. He stood on his own feet so firmly that he reared back."

But however smitten, the young man refused to play second fiddle to anything. "His very manliness," said Hurston, "sweet as it was, made us both suffer. My career balked the completeness of his ideal." Hurston did her best to conform to A.W.P.'s "ideal" of a dependent, clinging woman, but she could not become something she was not. "My work was one thing," she said, "and he was all the rest. But, I could not make him see that. Nothing must be in my life but himself."

A.W.P. begged Hurston to give up her career, marry him, and move away from New York. "I really wanted to do anything he wanted me to do," she wrote, "but that one thing I could not do." In the end, Hurston got her Guggenheim fellowship and sailed away to Jamaica. "This was my chance to release him," she said, "and fight myself free from my obsession."

In Jamaica, Hurston wrote later, "everywhere I set my feet down, there were tracks of blood. Blood from the very middle of my heart." She eased her pain by starting *Their Eyes Were Watching God*—in which, she said, "I tried to embalm all the tenderness of my passion for him."

After two months in New York, Hurston obtained a second Guggenheim and returned to Haiti to resume her study of voodoo. In late June, however, she suffered a severe gastric illness that sent her to bed for two weeks. Hurston was convinced that the sickness had been "sent"—perhaps through poisoned food—to dissuade her from continuing her investigations. Having seen numerous examples of voodoo priests' vengeance, she felt genuine fear for her life. Although she remained in Haiti for some months, she abandoned her collecting and concentrated on putting her notes in order. She returned to New York in late September, just in time for the publication of *Their Eyes Were Watching God*.

A masterpiece of American literature and Hurston's most celebrated novel, *Their Eyes Were Watching God* is the account of Janie Crawford's quest for self-realization. It is also a poignant love story, told in a lush and sensuous prose that often rises to pure poetry. Central to the novel is Hurston's study of the individual's struggle for self-knowledge and expression within the folk community, which both suffocates and empowers its members.

Janie Crawford's story begins when she is sixteen years old and intoxicated by the promise of a love she does not as yet understand. Her first two husbands seek to possess her body and soul, thus desecrating "the pear tree"—Hurston's symbol for the loving marriage of two free and equal souls. Only after the death of her second husband does Janie have the opportunity to follow her own inclinations. She falls in love and runs away with the young and spirited Vergible "Tea Cake" Woods, a man "who could be a bee to a blossom—a pear tree blossom in the spring."

Loving Janie for herself, Tea Cake wants only to share his life and have the opportunity to share hers. But he can be a male chauvinist too, and Janie must learn to insist upon her own rights, even as she grants him the right to be himself.

After Tea Cake's tragic death, Janie returns to Eatonville a whole woman, having experienced life and love for herself. As she tells her friend Phoeby, "You got tuh *go* there to *know* there. Yo papa and yo mama and nobody else can't tell yuh and show yuh. Two things everybody's got tuh do for theyselves. They got tuh go tuh God, and they got tuh find out about livin' fuh theyselves."

The critical response to *Their Eyes Were Watching God* continued the tradition established with *Mules and Men*. The *Saturday Review* called it a "rich and racy love story," although the magazine's reviewer expressed doubt that a place like Eatonville, "inhabited and governed entirely by Negroes," could exist. The *New York Post* said Hurston's "sensory" writing was on a par with that of D. H. Lawrence, the British author of such celebrated novels as *Lady Chatterley's Lover* and *Women in Love*. Another critic said Hurston's book was "simple and unpretentious," but

An impoverished family prepares for a meal in their home, a former schoolhouse in rural Georgia. Some black intellectuals assailed Hurston for not using her talent to depict lives

like these, using it instead to emphasize the positive side of southern black life. Said one New York critic, Hurston's work "should be more bitter."

added that "there is nothing quite like it."

Reactions from the black establishment, however, were largely negative and sometimes vicious. In a review for the leftist magazine *New Masses*, Richard Wright—the future author of *Native Son*—compared *Their Eyes Were Watching God* with a minstrel show, a bit of fluff designed to amuse white people. Accusing Hurston of exploiting the "quaint" aspects of black America, Wright said her novel carried "no theme, no message, no thought."

Hurston's longtime friend Alain Locke, at this point considered the dean of black scholars and critics, unleashed an even harsher blast at the novel. Although he conceded that Hurston possessed a "cradle-gift" for storytelling, he damned the book for emphasizing folklore and condescending to its characters. When, demanded Locke, would Hurston stop writing about "these pseudo-primitives who the reading public still loves to laugh with, weep over, and envy," and start writing "motive fiction and social document fiction?"

Plainly, black intellectuals were reviewing not the book Hurston had written but the book they *wished* she had written. Hurt and angered, particularly by Locke's shallow and cruel remarks about the complex, deeply felt work

Richard Wright, author of the classic novel Native Son, *came down hard on Hurston's* Their Eyes Were Watching God. *He accused her of trivializing black experience.*

she had created, Hurston unleashed a tirade. It was Locke, she said, who "condescended" to her characters by calling them "pseudo-primitives." His review, she raged, was "an example of rank dishonesty," written by a man who "pants to be a leader" but who "knows that he knows nothing about Negroes." *Opportunity* magazine, to which Hurston sent her furious response, declined to print it, but just composing the rebuttal probably made her feel a little better about Locke's attack.

Hurston spent the rest of the fall and winter putting her voodoo notes in order. Lippincott published the resulting volume, *Tell My Horse*, in 1938. An uneasy blend of travelogue and voodoo spiced with Hurston's photographs, the book received mixed notices. One critic called it a collection of "anthopological gossip"; another said, "The remembrances are vivid, the travelogue tedious..., and the anthropology a melange of misinterpretation and exceedingly good folklore."

Sales of *Tell My Horse* proved disappointing. More encouraging was an event that took place some months after its publication: in early June 1939, Hurston received an honorary Doctor of Letters degree from her old school, Morgan State College. She had other ceremonies on her mind as well: on June 27, she married again.

The forty-nine-year-old writer's second husband was Albert Price III, age twenty-three, a playground worker she had met in Florida. This marriage fared no better than her first. Hurston would later assert that Price drank heavily, abused her, and never worked. He, on the other hand, was to swear she had promised to support him and pay for his education. He also claimed that she threatened to "fix him" with a voodoo spell if he refused to obey her wishes. Because little is known of Price, the truth of the couple's accusations is almost impossible to verify; what is clear is that they spent most of their marriage apart. They were to divorce formally in 1943.

In November 1939, Hurston published *Moses, Man of the Mountain*, her third novel and fifth book in just seven years. Hurston, who had been working on the book for more than four years, hoped it would not only surpass the triumph of *Their Eyes Were Watching God* but would serve as a reply to those who had denounced her work for lacking contemporary social relevance.

Moses, Man of the Mountain is an audacious and ambitious book. In it, Hurston took it upon herself to redesign one of the most important stories of the Judeo-Christian tradition. During her investigations of black folklore and

voodoo, she had found a wealth of legends centered around the figure of Moses. As she wrote
in *Tell My Horse*, "wherever the Negro is
found, there are traditional tales of Moses and
his supernatural powers that are not in the
Bible." It was to this black tradition of Moses
as hero-hoodoo man that Hurston was
attracted.

Unlike the Bible's Moses, Hurston's Moses is
not a Jew but the son of an Egyptian princess.
Like the traditional Moses, he is the emissary
of God, but he is also a "conjure man," learned
in the ways of hoodoo. Although a divine voice
instructs him to lead the Jews out of Egyptian
slavery and into the Promised Land, Hurston
leaves open the possibility that the real owner
of the voice is not God but Jethro, a powerful
hoodoo man and Moses' teacher.

In Hurston's hands, the Jews' enslavement in
Egypt becomes the story of the black Africans
brought to the New World in bondage. Her
characters, who speak in several different
idioms, often express themselves in American
black dialect. When Jethro, for example, urges
Moses to rescue the Hebrews and teach them
about God, he says, "How about them
Israelites? They're down there in Egypt without
no god of their own and no more protection
than a bareheaded mule.... These people...need

help, Moses. And besides, we could convert 'em, maybe."

By turns hilarious, solemn, and deeply moving, Hurston's massive novel is filled with biting satire directed at both blacks and whites. Her treatment of the black struggle for freedom in *Moses, Man of the Mountain* assailed the current black leadership as sharply as it protested white oppression. Although Moses can lead the Jews out of slavery, he learns that "no man may make another free. Freedom was something internal. The outside signs were just signs and symbols of the man inside. All you could do was to give the opportunity for freedom and the man himself must make his own emancipation."

Moses received high praise from many white reviewers, but it was not the kind of protest novel Hurston's black critics had called on her to write. Once more, her work was attacked not for what it was, but for what it was not. Locke, for example, dismissed the book as "caricature," and Ralph Ellison (who would write *Invisible Man* in 1953) said, "For Negro fiction [*Moses, Man of the Mountain*] did nothing."

Among the novel's detractors was Hurston herself. "I don't think that I achieved all that I set out to do," she told a friend. "I thought that in this book I would achieve my ideal, but it seems that I have not yet reached it." Among recent literary observers, critic Blyden Jackson has perhaps characterized *Moses, Man of the Mountain* best, in words that apply as much to Hurston as to her work. The book, says Jackson, is "only life, actual, imperfect, sometimes difficult, and always true."

Hurston prepares to embark on one of her favorite pastimes, a fishing trip. Fulfilling a lifelong dream, the author bought herself a houseboat in 1943; she spent much of the next four years cruising Florida's lazy rivers and living at an integrated Daytona beach boatyard.

Chapter Nine

Dust Tracks

BY 1940, ZORA HURSTON was a nationally known figure. She had published two books about folklore, three novels, several short stories, and many newspaper and magazine articles. Her name had appeared in gossip and society columns, and she had been discussed and extensively interviewed in print and on the air.

But despite her fame, Hurston had never earned a substantial or even a dependable income from her books. In 1941, publisher Bertram Lippincott made a suggestion: hoping both to take advantage of the public's interest

This portrait of Hurston, taken by her friend Carl Van Vechten, vastly amused its subject. "I love myself when I am looking mean and impressive," she wrote.

in Hurston and to help her earn some money, he advised her to write her autobiography.

The idea had merit, for Hurston's life thus far had certainly been a rare adventure. Hurston, always secretive about her own history, greeted Lippincott's idea without enthusiasm, but she agreed to try. She wrote *Dust Tracks on a Road* during 1941 and early 1942, partly in New York and partly in California, where she worked briefly as a story consultant for Paramount Studios. The autobiography was published in November 1942, when Hurston was fifty-one years old.

Dust Tracks on a Road is a fascinating book that leaves out at least as much as it tells. Its early chapters, in which Hurston recounts her childhood in Eatonville and the hard years after her mother's death, are written with deep feeling and sparkling wit. Subsequent chapters contain an intriguing and unpredictable mixture of folk humor, philosophy, and personal observations. From the start, however, there are certain omissions of fact—Hurston's date of birth, for example—that grow more glaring as the book goes on.

The Harlem Renaissance is dismissed in a paragraph. *Jonah's Gourd Vine* receives a sentence or two; *Their Eyes Were Watching God* only a few more. *Moses, Man of the Mountain* is omitted entirely, as are the *Mule Bone* affair and Hurston's marriage to Albert Price. "I did not want to write [the book] at all," Hurston later confessed, "because it is too hard to reveal one's inner self."

In Hurston's original manuscript, she wrote at length and with some bitterness about the effects of American and European imperialism around the world; unfortunately, these comments were excised by her publisher as unpatriotic following America's 1941 entry into World War II. But the clear eye that Hurston could turn on international racism became somewhat clouded when she looked at the situation of blacks in the United States, and almost totally blind when she viewed her own situation. As literary observer Mary Helen Washington has observed, Hurston "could not depict blacks as defeated, humiliated, degraded, or victimized, because she did not experience black people or herself that way."

As Lippincott had predicted, the public loved *Dust Tracks*. The most popular book Hurston had ever written, it won the *Saturday Review*'s $1,000 Anisfield-Wolf Award for its contribution to "the field of race relations." Book reviewers raved over it; typical was the *New Yorker* magazine's critic, who called it a "warm, witty, imaginative, rich and winning

Gathering material for Mules and Men, *her 1935 treasury of black American folklore, Zora Neale Hurston listens to the music of a southern farmer. Writing later she would state:*

"*Negro folklore is not a thing of the past. It is still in the making. Its great variety shows the adaptability of the black man.*"

book by one of our few genuine, grade A folk writers."

Repeating the old pattern, many black critics disparaged *Dust Tracks*, suggesting that Hurston had written the book in order to please whites. Among these critics was novelist and critic Arna Bontemps, who wrote that "Miss Hurston deals very simply with the more serious aspects of Negro life in America—she ignores them."

That opinion was given weight by the 1943 publication of a newspaper interview with Hurston. A *New York Herald-Telegram* reporter quoted her as saying, "the lot of the Negro is much better in the South than in the North.... Of everything put up in the South for white people there is the equivalent for the Negro. In other words the Jim Crow system works."

Hurston was outraged when she read the interview. "I deny categorically that I ever said that Negroes were better off in the South," she fumed. "I am positively ill over it." What she had actually said, she pointed out in a letter to the reporter, was that "there was plenty of race prejudice both north and south," and that "there is a large body of Negroes in the South who...are wealthy, well-educated, and generally doing good for themselves."

But despite Hurston's denials, the damage was done. Roy Wilkins of the NAACP responded harshly: "Now is not the time for Negro writers like Zora Hurston to come out with publicity wisecracks about the South being better for the Negro than the North.... The race is fighting a battle that may determine its status for fifty years. Those who are not for us, are against us."

Hurston did not respond to Wilkins' blast directly, but she continued to insist that she did not "see life through the eyes of a Negro, but those of a person." She said, "I hate talking about the race problem. I am a writer, and leave sociological problems to sociologists, who know more about it than I do."

Despite this disclaimer, however, Hurston often wrote about race issues. During the war years (1941-45), she wrote numerous articles for such publications as the *Southern Literary Messenger*, the *American Mercury*, the *Saturday Evening Post*, and the *Negro Digest*. In these essays, she covered a wide range of subjects, including the war effort, black schools, and civil rights. In one of her articles, she lit into segregation.

"I am all for the repeal of every Jim Crow law in the nation here and now," she wrote in the *Negro Digest*. "Not in another generation or so. The Hurstons have already been waiting eighty years for that. I want it here and now.... I give my hand, my heart and my head to the total struggle."

In 1943, Hurston moved to Daytona Beach, Florida, and bought herself something else she had always wanted: a houseboat. Aboard this twenty-year-old, thirty-two-foot-long craft, the *Wanago*, she cruised the Indian and Halifax rivers, enjoying one of her all-time favorite pastimes, fishing. In March, she traveled briefly to Washington, D.C., to accept Howard University's annual Distinguished Alumni Award, but she preferred to remain in Florida aboard her beloved houseboat; there, she told a friend, "I have the solitude that I love."

Aboard her boat, Hurston continued to write—and continued to receive criticism from black intellectuals who said her works "do little credit to the Negro." Exasperated by the long-running complaint, Hurston was equally annoyed by the northerners she classified as "so-called liberals." These "'friends' of the Negro," she said, condescended to blacks by practicing a "sort of intellectual Jim Crow." They "seek out and praise [black people] of the lowest type and most sordid circumstances," she said, and then patronizingly pity the "poor Negro."

"I say to hell with it!" Hurston raged in a letter to a friend. "My back is broad. Let me, personally and privately, be responsible for my survival or failure to survive.... I want no double standards of measurement.... If I am a skunk, I meant to stink up the place.... If I am a walking rosebud, I did that too. I am a conscious being, all the plaints and pleas of the pressure groups inside and outside the race, to the contrary."

Between dashing off letters and magazine articles, Hurston was busily writing a new novel. Although she spent much of 1945 suffering from a painful intestinal illness, possibly related to the one she had suffered in Haiti, she finished the book, *Mrs. Doctor*, and sent it to Lippincott in September. To his dismay, the publisher saw a precipitous decline in Hurston's literary powers and regretfully rejected the novel. The book, about "the upper strata of Negro life," according to Hurston, was to remain unpublished.

Without the money she had expected from the sale of *Mrs. Doctor*, Hurston was again in need of funds. She traveled to New York, where she got a job working for Grant Reynolds, a conservative Republican running for a Harlem congressional seat. Reynolds lost the election, and Hurston remained in Harlem, in a state of deep depression, for the rest of the winter of 1946-47.

Hurston's depression stemmed in part from her lack of funds, which prevented her from going in search of new folklore. She had been planning an expedition to Honduras, hoping to discover a lost Mayan city and so end her financial worries at a single stroke. At last, in April 1947, Hurston got the chance to go. Thanks to the efforts of her friend Marjorie Kinnan Rawlings (author of *The Yearling*), the New York publishing house of Charles Scribner's Sons purchased the rights to Hurston's next book from J. B. Lippincott. With $500 from Scribner's in her pocket, Hurston sailed for Honduras on May 4, her spirits lifted by the prospect of new adventure.

Settling in the coastal town of Puerto Cortes, Hurston felt that she was once again her "old brash self." But instead of searching for lost cities, she began to work on her next novel, *Seraph on the Suwanee*. Scribner's accepted the book, and Hurston returned to New York in March 1948 for prepublication work. The novel was published in October 1948.

Unfortunately, the appearance of Hurston's first work of fiction in nearly a decade coincided with one of the most distressing events of

Publisher Bertram Lippincott gave Hurston one of the greatest thrills of her life when he wired his acceptance of her first novel, Jonah's Gourd Vine, *in 1933.*

her life. It had its roots in the winter of 1946, when she had lived in Harlem. Perceiving that her landlady's young son showed signs of serious mental illness, Hurston had—unwisely, as it turned out—suggested that his mother take him to a psychiatric clinic for testing. Apparently deeply insulted by the suggestion, the mother had brooded for more than a year.

When Hurston reentered the limelight with her new novel, the woman pounced: she formally charged Hurston (and two other adults, whom Hurston had never even met) with sexually molesting her son. New York policemen arrived at Hurston's apartment on September 13, 1948, and arrested her for committing an immoral act with a child. Dumbfounded, Hurston protested her innocence, even offering to take a lie-detector test, but she was indicted for the crime nonetheless.

Scribner's immediately hired a lawyer, who went to the district attorney with proof of his client's innocence: she had been in Honduras when the landlady's son had been allegedly molested. Realizing that the state had no case and that Hurston had been the victim of a disturbed accuser, the district attorney dropped all charges. But the damage done to Hurston's reputation—and to her state of mind—proved overwhelming. Although the white press had

Hurston spent the second half of 1947 in Honduras, where she lived at a hotel in Puerto Cortes and wrote her fourth novel, Seraph on the Suwanee.

ignored the story, several black newspapers had tried and convicted Hurston on their front pages.

Hurston felt she had been betrayed by her own people, and the effect was devastating. "I care nothing for anything anymore," she wrote to her friend Carl Van Vechten. "My country has failed me utterly. My race has seen fit to destroy me without reason, and with the vilest tools conceived of by man so far..., I feel hurled down a filthy privy hole."

It was in this bleak atmosphere that *Seraph on the Suwanee* appeared. Although Hurston was too upset to help promote the book, it sold extremely well. Nevertheless, most literary critics regard the novel as Hurston's least successful work. It is about poor Florida whites and contains only incidental appearances by black characters. Hurston had abandoned her traditional source of inspiration, the African-American cultural tradition, replacing it with an unconvincing world populated by women and men whose motivations often seem shadowy. *Seraph on the Suwanee* fails not because of its subject but because its characters never truly live.

On the strength of the novel's sales, Scribner's gave Hurston a $500 advance on her next book. With this money and the payments she received for several magazine articles, she lived comfortably in Florida for the next year and a half. By the spring of 1950, her new novel was still in progress but her money had run out. She decided to get a job—a decision that would make headlines.

"Famous Negro Author Working as Maid Here," blared the *Miami Herald* on March 27, 1950. Under a picture of Hurston, the paper revealed that the fifty-nine-year-old writer was currently employed as a domestic by a wealthy white woman in Miami. Hurston's employer, reported the *Herald*, had been reading the *Saturday Evening Post* one day when she happened to notice a familiar name: it was Zora Neale Hurston, the "girl" who was at that moment dusting her mistress' shelves.

The story, immediately flashed across the nation by the wire services, brought a flood of questions. Unwilling to admit she was working as a maid simply because she needed the money, Hurston told reporters she had wanted a break in her routine. "A writer has to stop writing every now and then and just live a little," she told one newspaperman. To another, she said she was planning to start a magazine for household workers, and that she had taken the job in order to learn "a great deal about a maid's life."

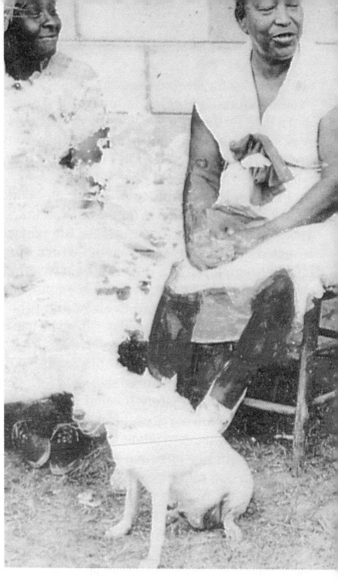

Hurston (center) chats with friends in Fort Pierce, Florida. Ill, overweight, and almost forgotten by the late 1950s, Hurston nonetheless retained her trademark optimism.

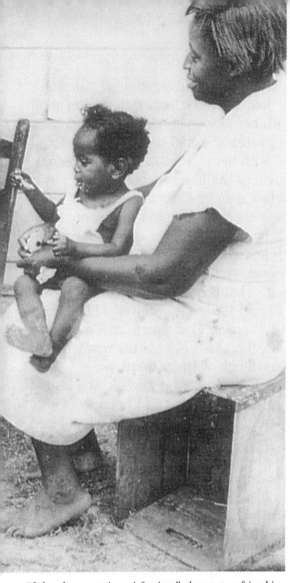

"I do take a certain satisfaction," she wrote a friend in 1957, *"in knowing that my writings are used in many of the great universities."*

Soon after the world learned of Hurston's domestic job, she left it, although still on good terms with her employer. Her former mistress told a reporter she had been surprised and delighted with her maid's "lack of pretensions, and a humility the like of which I have never encountered in an intelligent person."

For the next year, Hurston lived from hand to mouth on small sums she earned for magazine articles. During this period, she told a white friend, she was often "cold in hand," explaining, "That is a Negro way of saying penniless." In mid-1951, she received $1,000 for a *Saturday Evening Post* article and moved to Eau Gallie, the small Florida town where she had written much of *Mules and Men.*

There, for five dollars per week, she rented the same tiny house she had lived in twenty years earlier. She renovated the dilapidated building, planted a flower garden, and worked on a new novel, this one about the Bible's King Herod. As usual, she was very close to poverty, but as long as she could fish, garden, and feed herself and Spot, the little dog she had acquired, she was content. "Living the kind of life for which I was made, strenuous and close to the soil," she wrote to her Scribner's editor. "I am happier than I have been for at least ten years."

Tempering Hurston's happiness, however, was her health. She had begun to gain weight, and she suffered from an intestinal parasite she had picked up in Honduras. The parasitic infection left her aching and totally exhausted, sometimes for days at a time. But she kept on writing, energized by her vast enthusiasm for *Herod the Great.* "It is a whale of a story," she wrote a friend. "The struggle of a handful of Jews against the mightiest army on earth, that they might be free to live their own lives in their own way."

Unfortunately, Scribner's did not share her passion for *Herod.* In August 1955, her editor rejected the book, which he called "disappointing." Oddly calm about the rejection, Hurston wrote her editor a friendly note and began to expand the already immense manuscript, which was never to see publication.

To Hurston's sorrow, in the spring of 1956, her landlord sold the Eau Gallie cottage in which she had lived for five happy years. Just before she moved out, she went to Daytona Beach to collect an award for "education and human relations" from Bethune-Cookman College, where she had once briefly taught. For the next year, Hurston worked as a librarian at Patrick Air Force Base in Cocoa Beach, Florida.

In February 1958, Hurston moved to Fort Pierce, where she worked as a substitute teacher at Lincoln Park Academy. She supplemented her income with government unemployment checks and money for the freelance articles she wrote for the *Fort Pierce Chronicle*. Still working on *Herod*, she found her energy increasingly depleted by illness; at well over two hundred pounds, she was troubled by high blood pressure, an ulcer, and recurring stomach problems.

Hurston suffered a debilitating stroke in early 1959. Finally, in October, she was forced to enter the St. Lucie County Welfare Home. It was there, on January 28, 1960, that Zora Neale Hurston died of a heart attack just twenty-seven days after her sixty-ninth birthday. She was buried in an unmarked grave in the Garden of the Heavenly Rest, a segregated cemetery. It was hardly an appropriate final resting place for someone who took fierce pride in her black heritage yet insisted that "skins were no measure of what was inside people."

In 1973, writer Alice Walker placed a headstone on the grave. It features an epitaph from a poem by Jean Toomer that reads: "A Genius of the South."

But Hurston's genius stretched beyond any

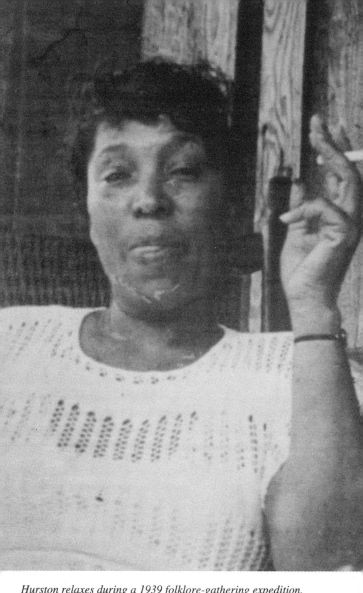

Hurston relaxes during a 1939 folklore-gathering expedition. "Zora was a cultural revolution simply because she was always herself," says Alice Walker.

one place and time. In *Dust Tracks on a Road*, she wrote—almost as though she had been penning her own epitaph:

> I know that nothing is destructible; things merely change forms. When the consciousness we know as life ceases, I know I shall still be part and parcel of the world.... Why fear? The stuff of my being is...ever changing, ever moving, but never lost....
>
> I have known the joy and pain of deep friendship. I have served and been served. I have made some good enemies for which I am not a bit sorry. I have loved unselfishly, and I have fondled hatred with the red-hot tongs of Hell. That's living.

INDEX

PICTURE CREDITS

Alain Locke Papers, Moorland-Spingarn Research Center, Howard University: pp. 19, 68-69, 77, 135; Courtesy Ms. Altermese Smith Bentley: pp. 20, 23; The Bettmann Archive: pp. 11, 32-33, 89, 91, 154-155, 157, 177; Courtesy Carl Van Vechten Estate: pp. 8, 13, 163, 164; University of Florida Library: pp. 42, 180-181; Erik Overbey Collection, University of Southern Alabama: pp. 96, 106-107; Florida State Archives, pp. 29, 46-47; Robert Hemenway: p. 51; Jane Belo Estate, p. 146; Photo by Stetson Kennedy, print courtesy of University of Florida Library: p. 185; Library of Congress: pp. 25, 101, 168-169; Courtesy of the Lippincott Family: p. 175; The Schomburg Center for Research in Black Culture, The New York Public Library, Astor, Lenox and Tilden Foundations: pp. 65, 80-81, 136; Sheen Educational Foundation Library and the University of Florida Library: p. 75; Special Collections Library, Morgan State University: pp. 54-55; UPI/Bettman Archive: pp. 62, 84-85, 92-93; Courtesy of Mrs. Wright, reprinted by permsision of John Hawkins and Associates, Inc., print from Bettman Archive: p. 157; Langston Hughes Estate: p. 110; Ray Locke: pp. 112, 116-117, 120-121, 124-125, 128-129.